Register Your Book

at ibmpressbooks.com/ibmregister

Upon registration, we will send you electronic sample chapters from two of our popular IBM Press books. In addition, you will be automatically entered into a monthly drawing for a free IBM Press book.

Registration also entitles you to:

- Notices and reminders about author appearances, conferences, and online chats with special guests
- Access to supplemental material that may be available
- Advance notice of forthcoming editions
- Related book recommendations
- Information about special contests and promotions throughout the year
- Chapter excerpts and supplements of forthcoming books

Contact us

If you are interested in writing a book or reviewing manuscripts prior to publication, please write to us at:

Editorial Director, IBM Press
c/o Pearson Education
800 East 96th Street
Indianapolis, IN 46240

e-mail: IBMPress@pearsoned.com

Visit us on the Web: ibmpressbooks.com

Related Books of Interest

Search Engine Marketing, Inc.
Driving Search Traffic to Your Company's Web Site

by Mike Moran and Bill Hunt
ISBN: 0-13-606868-5

The #1 Step-by-Step Guide to Search Marketing Success...Now Completely Updated with New Techniques, Tools, Best Practices, and Value-Packed Bonus DVD!

Thoroughly updated to fully reflect today's latest search engine marketing opportunities, this book guides you through profiting from social media marketing, site search, advanced keyword tools, hybrid paid search auctions, and much more. You'll walk step-by-step through every facet of creating an effective program: projecting business value, selling stakeholders and executives, building teams, choosing strategy, implementing metrics, and above all, execution.

Do It Wrong Quickly
How the Web Changes the Old Marketing Rules

by Mike Moran
ISBN: 0-13-225596-0

For decades, marketers have been taught to carefully plan ahead because "you must get it right–it's too expensive to change." But, in the age of the Web, you can know in hours whether your strategy's working. Today, winners don't get it right the first time: They start fast, change fast, and relentlessly optimize their way to success. They do it wrong quickly...then fix it, just as quickly!

In this book, Internet marketing pioneer Mike Moran shows you how to do that—step-by step and in detail. Drawing on his experience building ibm.com into one of the world's most successful sites, Moran shows how to quickly transition from "plan then execute" to a nonstop cycle of refinement. You'll master specific techniques for making the Web's "two-way marketing conversation" work successfully, productively, and profitably. Next, Moran shows how to choose the right new marketing tools, craft them into an integrated strategy, and execute it...achieving unprecedented efficiency, accountability, speed, and results.

 Listen to the author's podcast at:
ibmpressbooks.com/podcasts

Related Books of Interest

Multisite Commerce
Proven Principles for Overcoming the Business, Organizational, and Technical Challenges

by Lev Mirlas
ISBN: 0-13-714887-9

Plan, Manage, and Architect Multiple Web Sites for Maximum Efficiency and Business Value.

In *Multisite Commerce*, Lev Mirlas—the architect who pioneered the concept of a shared multisite platform with IBM WebSphere Commerce—introduces best practices and methodologies for implementing and managing multiple e-commerce sites efficiently and cost-effectively.

This book's start-to-finish methodology provides a common language that everyone involved in multiple sites—from executives to project managers and technical architects to site administrators—can share.

The Social Factor
Innovate, Ignite, and Win through Mass Collaboration and Social Networking

by Maria Azua
ISBN: 0-13-701890-8

Companies are increasingly investing in social networks. However, they routinely miss powerful opportunities to drive value and promote innovation by using social networking to build thriving communities of employees, partners, and customers. In *The Social Factor,* IBM vice president Maria Azua shows how to do just that— and gain a powerful competitive edge.

Azua draws on her experience guiding the successful deployment of multiple social networking solutions to more than 300,000 IBM employees and customers worldwide. From her unique perspective as a strategist and technology thought leader, she assesses each of today's most powerful social technologies including blogs, wikis, tag clouds, social media, social search, virtual worlds, and even smart phones.

Listen to the author's podcast at:
ibmpressbooks.com/podcasts

Related Books of Interest

Web 2.0 and Social Networking for the Enterprise
Guidelines and Examples for Implementation and Management Within Your Organization
by Joey Bernal
ISBN: 0-13-700489-3

The Hands-On Guide to Thriving with Web 2.0 and Social Networking.

This book provides hands-on, start-to-finish guidance for business and IT decision-makers who want to drive value from Web 2.0 and social networking technologies. IBM expert Joey Bernal systematically identifies business functions and innovations these technologies can enhance and presents best-practice patterns for using them in both internal—and external-facing applications. Drawing on the immense experience of IBM and its customers, Bernal addresses both the business and technical issues enterprises must manage to succeed. He offers insights and case studies covering multiple technologies, including AJAX, REST, Atom/RSS, enterprise taxonomies, tagging, folksonomies, portals, mashups, blogs, wikis, and more.

The New Language of Marketing 2.0
Carter
ISBN: 0-13-714249-8

The New Language of Business
Carter
ISBN: 0-13-195654-X

The Greening of IT
Lamb
ISBN: 0-13-715083-0

Eating the IT Elephant
Hopkins and jenkins, Kreulen
ISBN: 0-13-713012-0

Mining the Talk
Spangler, Kreulen
ISBN: 0-13-233953-6

Viral Data in SOA
Fishman
ISBN: 0-13-700180-0

Enterprise Master Data Management
Dreibelbis, Hechler, Milman, Oberhofer, van Run, Wolfson
ISBN: 0-13-236625-8

Audience, Relevance, and Search

Audience, Relevance, and Search

Targeting Web Audiences with Relevant Content

James Mathewson   **Frank Donatone**   **Cynthia Fishel**

IBM Press

Pearson plc

Upper Saddle River, NJ • Boston • Indianapolis • San Francisco

New York • Toronto • Montreal • London • Munich • Paris • Madrid

Capetown • Sydney • Tokyo • Singapore • Mexico City

ibmpressbooks.com

The authors and publisher have taken care in the preparation of this book, but make no expressed or implied warranty of any kind and assume no responsibility for errors or omissions. No liability is assumed for incidental or consequential damages in connection with or arising out of the use of the information or programs contained herein.

IBM Press Program Managers: Steve Stansel, Ellice Uffer
Cover design: IBM Corporation

Associate Publisher: Greg Wiegand
Marketing Manager: Kourtnaye Sturgeon
Publicist: Heather Fox
Acquisitions Editor: Bernard Goodwin
Managing Editor: John Fuller
Designer: Alan Clements
Project Editor: Elizabeth Ryan
Copy Editor: Ed Winograd
Indexer: Ted Laux
Compositor: LaserWords
Proofreader: Mike Shelton
Manufacturing Buyer: Dan Uhrig

Publishing as IBM Press

IBM Press offers excellent discounts on this book when ordered in quantity for bulk purchases or special sales, which may include electronic versions and/or custom covers and content particular to your business, training goals, marketing focus, and branding interests. For more information, please contact:

> U. S. Corporate and Government Sales
> 1-800-382-3419
> corpsales@pearsontechgroup.com.

For sales outside the U. S., please contact:

> International Sales
> international@pearson.com

The following terms are trademarks or registered trademarks of International Business Machines Corporation in the United States, other countries, or both: IBM, the IBM logo, IBM Press, BladeCenter, and DB2. Microsoft, Bing, and Windows Live are trademarks of the Microsoft Corporation in the United States, other countries, or both. Flash is a registered trademark of Adobe Systems Incorporated in the United States, other countries, or both. JavaScript is a trademark of Sun Microsystems, Inc. in the United States, other countries or both. Other company, product, or service names may be trademarks or service marks of their respective owners.

Library of Congress Cataloging-in-Publication Data
Mathewson, James, 1963–
    Audience, relevance, and search : targeting Web audiences with relevant content / James Mathewson, Frank Donatone, Cynthia Fishel.
        p.   cm.
    Includes index.
    ISBN-13: 978-0-13-700420-1 (pbk. : alk. paper)
    ISBN-10: 0-13-700420-6 (pbk. : alk. paper)
  1. Online authorship.   2. Web usage mining.   3. Web sites—Design.   4. Web search engines.   5. Internet users.   6. Internet marketing.   I. Donatone, Frank.   II. Fishel, Cynthia.   III. Title.
    PN171.O55M38 2010
    006.3—dc22   2010006751

        Pearson Education, Inc.
        Rights and Contracts Department
        501 Boylston Street, Suite 900
        Boston, MA 02116
        Fax: (617) 671-3447

ISBN-13: 978-0-13-700420-1
ISBN-10:   0-13-700420-6

Text printed in the United States on recycled paper at Courier in Stoughton, Massachusetts.
First printing, April 2010

To my wife Beth, who endured many late nights and lonely weekends as I sat tapping away in the office. Without her love and care I would not have had the strength to do this. Also to my son John, who was always there with a smile and a few words of encouragement as I explained to him that I couldn't play catch or go for a bike ride with him because I had to write.

—James Mathewson

To my wife Gail, for her love, encouragement, and confidence in me. To my son Tom, for showing me that success can be found on the road less traveled.

—Frank Donatone

To my children Eliana and Jason, with great appreciation for their support for me. A very special acknowledgment and thanks to Joel Leitner for his tremendous patience, encouragement, and support.

—Cynthia Fishel

Contents

Sidebars

Foreword

Although in recent years the Internet has been overrun with images, audio, and video, the Web remains, at its heart, a writer's medium.

Why do I say this? Because the written word is at the heart of every Web experience. No matter how much video you watch, images you look at, and audio you listen to, you read a lot more words. While Web sites demand skilled people to create all of these kinds of content, the demand for Web writers has never been greater.

And that demand keeps growing, both because more companies each day are using the Web as a marketing tool, and because messages are virtually unlimited in size. Unlike every other medium, there is no natural limit to the amount of space that can be used for a Web message. Advertising increases in cost as size goes up. Direct mail costs increase for paper and stamps. On the Web, the words can just go on and on with almost no incremental cost—you can always create one more page that explains one more idea.

So, yes, it's a writer's medium. But not just any writer need apply. If you are an accomplished writer, schooled in creating advertising copy, magazine articles, direct mail pieces, newspaper stories, books, or any other kind of printed media, you have the basic skills required to succeed on the Web. But you don't have *all* the skills you need.

The book you hold in your hands can help any experienced writer adapt those skills for Web writing. Web writing is a challenge for even the most gifted print writer, for several reasons.

- **Web writers must be brief.** The act of reading on an electronic device causes readers to skim content rather then read in depth. Even though this user behavior might change over time, as people get more used to reading from a computer screen, the relatively cramped experience of reading from mobile devices will always demand brevity for online writers. While you can always create another page, you must be brief and to the point within each page.

- **Web writers must appeal to search engines.** Because Google and other search engines are so important in driving traffic to Web sites, no writer can afford to overlook search engines as an audience equally important as Web users. While many elements go into successful search marketing, the words on the page are the most important.

- **Web writers must create pass-alongs.** Web sites have always needed links from other sites, and well-written content makes that happen. Nowadays, social media allows customers to pass along good content to other Web users, using blogs, Twitter, social networks, and many other means. This new stream of minute-by-minute content creates a nearly endless demand for good writers.

If you are feeling a bit overwhelmed at the thought of adapting your writing style for all of these new demands, don't be. This book leads you through these concepts, and many more, in step-by-step fashion. The authors are experts in the practical approaches needed to succeed as a Web writer for any company.

You'll learn everything, from determining the relevance of your message to your audience, through measuring the results of your efforts. You'll especially learn how to use search engines and social media to ensure that your message is seen by the maximum possible audience.

Don't assume that everything you know about writing is wrong when it comes to the Web. It's not. You need not be intimidated from branching out to this new online medium. But neither should you assume that there's nothing to learn. This book will help you leverage the writing skills you've always had to enter the brave new world of Web writing success. So stop reading this foreword and dive into what you really need to know!

—Mike Moran
Author of *Do It Wrong Quickly*
Coauthor of *Search Engine Marketing, Inc.*

Preface

Many books focus on how to publish content on the Web, or how to measure its success, or how to take existing text from print venues and make it suitable for the Web. But no book adequately focuses on creating text exclusively for the Web. Perhaps everyone thinks that the topic of writing has been adequately covered in such works as Strunk and White's excellent little book, *The Elements of Style, Third Edition* (1979). Our view is that this assumption misses an important fact: Writing for the Web is fundamentally different from writing for print. We will unpack this fact to delve into how to write successfully for the Web.

In so doing, we fill an important gap in the literature. Other books about Web publishing, such as Mike Moran and Bill Hunt's book *Search Engine Marketing Inc., Second Edition* (2009), focus on using the Web medium as a marketing tool, but spend only a few pages on the key success factor on the Web: writing. The old saying "content is king" rings ever clearer as the Web evolves. Search engines such as Google, and social media venues such as Facebook, accentuate the need for Web-centric writing. This book helps its readers write effectively for the Web by taking into account how search and social media usage affect readership and audience. This is not just a challenge; it's an opportunity. Search and social media can help Web writers learn common audience attitudes to better engage their audience with relevant content.

The target audience for this book includes writers, editors, and content strategists. Though many of the examples and case studies apply to Web marketing (the field in which the authors have 45 years of accumulated Web experience), the book is intended to have a broader scope than just marketing writing. Writers for blogs, wikis, and various online media outlets can also benefit from the insights contained in this book. Web marketing is just an excellent source of rich Web publishing examples, because it clearly shows how effective writing has changed on the Web.

In print media, readers have already chosen to pick up the publication. This simple act implies a certain level of consent as to its relevance. Print writers can assume that the reader finds the publication at least nominally relevant and can get on with the business of presenting a compelling flow of information. But on the Web, visitors often don't choose the specific page they land on through search or social media referrals. They must first determine the relevance of the page to their needs. For this reason, Web writers must demonstrate relevance before they can start engaging Web visitors in the flow of information. This step is often missed by Web writers, who wonder why so many Web visitors leave their pages without engaging in the content at all. This book shows writers, editors, and content strategists how to attract a target audience to content that is relevant to them, how to demonstrate this relevance when their target audience arrives on the site, and how to measure the depth of the audience's engagement.

After an introductory chapter, the book spends the next two chapters discussing foundational concepts about how print and Web media differ. It focuses on how relevance determination and audience analysis differ on the Web, as opposed to print. This is necessarily deep stuff, because it depends on a rich body of literature in three different fields. We do not want to present the literature in a breezy fashion, out of respect for the great minds who have studied media determinism, relevance theory, and audience analysis over the centuries. Still, we do our best to make the topics accessible to those without backgrounds in these fields.

After the fundamentals are covered, Chapters 4 and 5 focus on how to write for the Web using a search-first perspective. Search-first writing is based on the premise that search engines provide a lot of insights into what is relevant to your target audience. Unpacking this assumption is central to this book.

This discussion has two major themes. The first theme relates to word choice: If you know what words resonate with your target audience members, you can write more effectively for them. You learn these words through keyword and social media research. The second theme is the subject of Chapters 6 and 7: how links determine the structure of Web information. Search engines use links to determine the relevance and credibility of content on the Web. They then use that information to sort search engine results for their users—the writers' audience. Designing your site (Chapter 6) and collaborating with other sites to enable search engines to determine the relevance and credibility of your content (Chapter 7) are writing tasks unique to Web publishing. Some of the insights developed in these chapters are unique to this book.

The Web is a social medium—ever more so with new applications that connect like-minded people to communities centered on conversations. This is not a new phenomenon: The Web has always had a social element, as the value of Web content is directly proportional to the quantity and quality of links to it. The best way to get links to your content is by collaborating with the community of experts in your topics of interest. This is as true for traditional static Web pages as it is on Facebook. Still, there are aspects of social media writing that differ from traditional Web publishing. Chapter 8 delves into these distinctions.

Unlike print publications, Web sites are never done. The more you change them to accommodate your audience, the more effective they become. Measuring site effectiveness and making intelligent changes to better adapt to audience needs is the subject of Chapter 9.

Though we must call this book done and published, the Web will continue to evolve, requiring our continued updates and new insights. We will add to the gift of knowledge this book represents by maintaining a related Web site (www.writingfordigital.com) containing blog posts around our particular areas of expertise and links to the references you will find in our bibliography.

The Story of This Book

This book had its genesis in my M.S. thesis of the same title in scientific and technical communication at the University of Minnesota. When the thesis was published in August of 2008, I was collaborating with Frank Donatone and Cynthia Fishel on five search engine optimization courses for writers, editors, and content strategists at IBM. Education was part of my role as editor-in-chief of ibm.com. Frank and Cynthia brought fresh examples of the best practices to our course development as they consulted with their clients as Web effectiveness leads. The concept of marrying the content in the thesis with the coursework to create a comprehensive book on search-first writing for the Web was mutually agreeable to us.

What we didn't realize when we entered into the coauthoring relationship was how much we would learn along the journey of writing this book. Like a jigsaw puzzle emerging before our eyes, the missing pieces presented themselves as fresh insights amidst the lessons we taught in our search courses. We could not have predicted the almost daily eureka moments as we wrote page after page and chapter after chapter. We hope you enjoy reading this book as much as we enjoyed writing it.

—James Mathewson
Faribault, Minnesota

Acknowledgments

The writing of this book was an odyssey. Along the way, numerous people helped us create something that transcends the collective skills of the coauthors. These folks fall into two rough categories: professional colleagues who helped with drafts of the proposal or reviews of the chapters, and friends and family members who provided the kind of support only those who are closest to us can give. Here, we thank our colleagues and dedicate this book to those close to us.

Special thanks:

- We are grateful to Mike Moran and Bill Hunt for guiding our proposal writing so that this book complements their own, rather than competing with it. We are especially grateful to Mike for writing the foreword.

- We are grateful to those who directed us through the publishing process, especially Bernard Goodwin, Michelle Housley, and Steve Stansel.

- We are grateful to Klaus Rusch, Daniele Hayes, Chris Williams, Jennette Banks, and Daria Goetsch for their very helpful review comments.

- We are grateful to our IBM managers, especially Klaus Rusch and Charles Chesnut, for letting this book eat a portion of our brains for more than a year.

- We are grateful to our mentors, named and unnamed, who counseled us through the ups and downs of the writing process. The authors received valuable mentorship from Aaron Dibernardo and Dave Evans.

- James is especially grateful to Professor Billie Wahlstrom for advising the M.S. thesis project that ultimately led to this book; and to Monica Piccinni, who mentored him through the writing process.

- Cynthia is especially grateful to Richard Kelley, who mentored her through the writing process and encouraged the writing of this book.

About the Authors

James Mathewson has followed the Web since 1994, first as a contributing editor specializing in Web publishing and search for *ComputerUser* magazine, and later as the editor-in-chief of the magazine and its Web site. As the ComputerUser.com editor, he published more than one thousand articles, mostly related to Web technologies. He has also published in several other magazines and periodicals, including IBM Systems magazines.

Since leaving *ComputerUser* in 2004, James has worked for IBM as a Web developer and Web content editor. In his current role as editor-in-chief of ibm.com, James sets standards, and creates and delivers education to improve the effectiveness of IBM's Web content. James has trained more than one thousand writers, editors, and content strategists on Web content quality and search engine optimization (SEO) within IBM. James leads all search effectiveness efforts for IBM's Smarter Planet Web presence (ibm.com/smarterplanet). He is also the search strategy lead for IBM Marketing and Communications, a role that gives him influence over future Web and social media content efforts at IBM.

James has two masters degrees from the University of Minnesota. His M.A. in the philosophy of language and linguistics focused on the relationship between meaning and relevance in language. His M.S. in scientific and technical communication focused on the relationship between audience analysis and relevance in the Web medium.

James lives in Faribault, Minnesota, with his wife Beth, son John, and dog Sophie. In his spare time, he works at his wife's coffee shop as the coffee cupper and buyer. He also sings in two church choirs and attempts to make music on his guitar. James enjoys all forms of motorless outdoor recreation.

Frank Donatone is an internet professional with more than twenty years' experience in the IT industry. His experience includes people management, project management, Web design, usability, accessibility, search engine marketing with a SEMPO certification in advanced SEO, and social media optimization. Using his previous experience in addition to customer satisfaction survey analysis he provides tactical and strategic recommendations to IBM for Web site improvement. His position as an IBM Worldwide Web Effectiveness Lead has a strong focus on SEO and social media to improve IBM's ranking on the Web for key terms, managing the brand's reputation, identifying sales opportunities, and improving share of voice. Frank has also codeveloped and taught several search engine optimization courses at IBM with his coauthors. Recently, he has participated in the design and presentation of education related to using social media for sales inclusive of Twitter, LinkedIn, and event promotion. In addition to his Web Effectiveness role Frank also serves as a social media lead for ibm.com.

Prior to joining IBM Frank was an IT consultant to IBM as well as a second-line manager for Keane Inc. accounts at three IBM sites, *Readers Digest*, and VSI Communications. His second-line management position encompassed the management of 4 first-line account managers and 50 consultants. His dual role as a consultant at IBM during this tenure was Lotus Notes help desk management and Lotus Notes and Web application deployment quality assurance. He also holds a professional certification in Lotus Notes administration and development.

Frank currently lives in Eastchester, New York, with his wife Gail, son Tom, and parrotlet Lucille. Frank can be reached through LinkedIn at www.linkedin.com/in/donatone.

Cynthia Fishel is a senior interactive marketing and brand specialist with more than twenty-four years of global agency and corporate *Fortune* 500 experience in the IT Industry. She has a proven track record of building teams that build successful Web sites. She was part of the original team that launched ibm.com back in the early '90s and has continued to work on IBM's Web site for the past fifteen years. She produced the ibm.com Interactive and Visual Design Standards in support of all ibm.com worldwide Web development for consistent customer experiences. She drove IBM's strategy for Web collaboration and developed the first Collaborative Branding Standards for comarketed and cobranded Web sites.

Cynthia was part of the IBM team that set standards, and created and delivered education to improve the effectiveness of IBM's Web content. As a Search and Social Media evangelist for IBM with a SEMPO certification in advance SEO, Cynthia led the development of multiple organic SEO education modules for use by IBM internally, IBM Business Partners, and interactive agencies, used to train thousands of associates worldwide.

Cynthia spearheaded other ibm.com initiatives and education in Corporate Identity & Design, Digital Branding, Rich Media, Accessibility, and Privacy. As an IBM Worldwide Web Effectiveness Lead she was the single point of contact for IBM business units, helping them better attract, convert, and retain business through the Web. She is currently a vice president/director at Digitas/Publicis Groupe, responsible for interactive marketing, branding, and SEO initiatives supporting the world's largest electronics company.

In addition to her search and social media work, Cynthia holds a Preparatory Department Certificate from the University of Rochester's Eastman School of Music, a Bachelors of Music in piano with high distinction from Indiana University, and an M.A. in business administration from New York University. Cynthia lives in Bedford, New York, with her son and daughter and can be reached through LinkedIn at www.linkedin.com/in/cynthiafishel.

Writing for Web Users Implies Writing for Search Engines

Writing for the Web is fundamentally different than writing for other media, such as print. Sure, some good writing habits for print also apply to the Web. You should use an engaging tone and fresh word choices. You should organize your information clearly. And, most importantly, you should understand your audiences and write in ways that make it easy for them to understand your content. However, analysis shows that readers approach Web content far differently than print content. This book seeks to use this insight to provide a practical guide for Web writers and content strategists.

This book is about understanding the content needs of Web users to do a better job of presenting relevant content to them. It assumes a good working knowledge of how to write for print and therefore will not delve into the mechanics of quality writing. But it *will* focus on the distinction between how print and Web media differ, which requires some explanation of how the print medium works. From this foundation, we can understand how the Web as a medium differs from print. We can then develop practical guidance on how to do a better job of engaging Web readers.

You might be skeptical about this. Whether for Web or print, text is text, right? In this book, it is our job to counter this skepticism. In subsequent chapters we will cite numerous case studies and deep research into user behavior that clearly demonstrate how Web readers behave and why they do. For the time being, however, we ask that you suspend your skepticism so that we can introduce the content of this book. What follows is a brief sketch of the chapters in this book, which we hope will convince you to read on. We promise that by understanding what is covered in these chapters, you can truly master a field that is crying out for competent practitioners: Web content writing.

How the Web Medium Has Evolved from Its Print Origins

The basic difference between print and Web media is in the reader/writer relationship. In print contexts, you typically invite an audience to journey with you through your prescribed content path. The best print writers encourage their readers to surrender control and let the writer lead them by the hand through the material. Often, print readers will readily concede this control, trusting that the writer knows how best to organize and present information.

On the Web, readers (if we may call them readers for the present) will not cede control over the information path. They navigate through paths of their choosing, cutting corners and trying to get to the most relevant content as quickly as possible. On the Web, it is the writer's job to provide a multitude of clearly marked paths, letting readers find the relevant nuggets of information that they seek. How to write to let readers sift through your content and find those nuggets is a considerable challenge that deserves a book of its own.

A particularly salient example of how Web writing differs from print is the way Web readers use search engines. Web users are impatient with content providers, because they can be. If they can't find the information they're looking for by navigating to it, they will use search engines. This impatience with information retrieval shows up in their reading habits. As a study of Web users by Weinreich et al. (February 2008) has demonstrated, Web "readers" do much more skimming and scanning than print readers. The study shows that on average, people spend 82% less time actually *reading* Web pages than they do when they read print pages, assuming average print reading speeds of 250 words per minute.

As Jakob Nielsen (June 2008) shows, Web users usually don't read pages in the conventional way, line by line, serially. They scan for keywords in the heading and short descriptions and only read after deciding that some content is relevant. With this in mind, Google has designed its search crawler to mimic how Web users behave. The crawler scans pages for keywords and captures the pages with the strongest placement of those keywords to include in its index. When a user enters a keyword phrase into Google's search field, Google returns the results that its algorithm deems relevant to those search terms. The design of its crawler is one reason that Google has become the search engine market leader in the United States and elsewhere. It tends to return highly relevant results for users, and it displays those results in ways that users can easily digest, given their extreme impatience. Because Google and other search engines strongly cater to Web user behavior, learning to write for the Google algorithm is an essential aspect of writing for Web readers.

Though our book relies on much of the information provided in Mike Moran's and Bill Hunt's excellent book *Search Engine Marketing, Inc., Second Edition* (2009), this is one point where our approach diverges from theirs. Hunt and Moran claim (2005, 309) that "The best philosophy for writing for search is: Write for people first, not for search engines." Our claim is that writing for search engines approximates writing for people. Also, Web writers often lack audience knowledge—readers can come from anywhere using search. Because Web writers often lack audience knowledge, writing for search engines is often the best way to understand how to write for people. So we take a "write-for-search-engines-first" approach.

Writing Relevant Content for the Web Audience

How do you analyze your audience for print publications? Suppose you write for academic periodicals. If so, you have a good sense of the history of debate within each one. And you know that readers of a given periodical are professors or graduate students in the field. Perhaps you have a demographic survey of its subscribers. From this, you form a mental representation of a typical reader (maybe even someone you know, like your advisor), and as you write or review your own work, you imagine that person reading it. In the print world, this is the closest you will ever get to addressing audience members based on known facts about them.

In most print contexts, you know significantly less about your audience than you do in academic periodical contexts. Magazine writers might know rough demographics about subscribers, but they never know who might pick up a given publication at newsstands. Book writers know even less about their audiences. You might write a book for a particular audience, in the sense that you define its topic and purpose so that audience members who are interested in those things will buy it or check it out. But you don't always know exactly how to address them, either as individuals or as a group. Print audiences are typically much more diverse than subscribers to an academic journal. It is simply not possible to address all possible readers with one print product. You just don't know them well enough to do this.

For this reason, many print writers invoke their audiences by using storytelling and other compelling techniques to draw them into the book's world. When readers start down the path of a particular story, they leave all expectations of being addressed for who they are at the trail head and follow the writer into unexplored territory. The more richly the writer creates that territory, the more readers will feel compelled to take the journey.

On the Web, you know a little more about your audiences, but your knowledge is fairly generic: You might know their service providers and perhaps which search engines they came from, and which paths they take through your site. But on an individual level, you don't know much at all. (Unless they sign in to your site. But let's leave those cases behind, since very few users take the time to do so. And even if they do sign in, what you know about them can't help you tailor messages for them.) Because users take unpredictable paths through your information, you can't connect with your audience as you do in print, such as by addressing a tightly defined audience or by appealing to a diverse audience. You have to find some way to connect with them in order to deliver content that they will find relevant. There are no perfect solutions to this problem, but we have developed some strategies and tactics to help you better connect with anonymous audiences on the Web. All of them center on search.

When you write content explicitly for search engines rather than for your users, in a sense, you invoke the search engine users with an effective mix of keywords and links that draws them to your pages. The challenge is to craft your pages in ways that attract specific users from search engines, especially Google. In so doing, you can present relevant information to your audience. This book is about attracting your audience with keywords and links and thereby providing relevant information to them. As mentioned earlier, because Google and other search engines cater to the way users scan and retrieve content on the Web, writing for Google is also an effective way to write relevant content for your audience.

Discovering and Using Popular Keywords

The first thing to do if you want to optimize your pages for search is to find out what keywords related to your theme or topic are most often searched for. These keywords become your site's nomenclature. If you use these words in prominent ways on pages in your site, you will have a better chance to get traffic.

But traffic volume is not the end game. The end game is *targeted* traffic. You want to engage with your visitors. You want your target audience to come to your site and find that your content is relevant to them. Visitors who find your content irrelevant typically click the back button or "bounce" off your site without clicking any of its links. If you try to get high traffic without taking care to also target your audience in the process, you will get a lot of traffic; but most of it will bounce. What you want, instead, is low bounce rates with relatively high traffic. How can you achieve this? It's not as easy as it might seem. Popular keywords that are used by many people in a variety of contexts will yield mixed results, if all you do is optimize your pages for those keywords. You will get high traffic volume, but also high bounce rates. The first step is to develop a set of related keywords—or a **keyword cloud**—which your target audience uses frequently. Then you need to develop pages that use the words in this cloud.

So how do you develop these keyword clouds? One way is to use keyword research tools to find related keywords. These tools can help you identify not only the most often searched-on words, but also related words and how often they are searched on. Once you get a sense for the number of users who search on a keyword—or its search demand—you can use the most relevant, high-demand words as the building blocks for your content.

When we use the term *keyword*, we do not merely refer just to single words. Most keywords that users enter into search engines consist of *phrases*. A keyword cloud typically contains not only related single words, but also related phrases. Many users search on so-called **long-tail keywords** to zero in on the exact content they are looking for. These are not just longer strings of words and phrases, though they typically are longer than high-demand single words. The phrase **long-tail** refers to the demographics of users who search for very *particular* content, rather than searching on more *generic* topics. Users who enter long-tail queries tend to be more search savvy. If your content ranks well for these, you will attract a highly targeted audience. But no single long tail will garner much traffic. The number of long-tail keywords in your content will need to be enough to drive targeted traffic to your site. For these keywords, you have to understand the language of your target audience at the *sentence* level, rather than at the *phrase* level. One way to develop this understanding is to research your target audience's social media hangouts, such as blogs, communities, and forums. Because users tend to use the same sentences in their long-tail keyword searches that they use in social media contexts, knowing the writing habits of your target audience will help you know the best long-tail keywords to use.

There are a variety of tools you can use to better understand the writing habits of your target audience. Very effective ways to do this include Google Alerts, Yahoo Alerts, and a method that uses Yahoo Pipes to track mentions of your company via **RSS feeds**—subscription feeds that automatically update when the source content is changed. You can use these methods to guarantee that whenever someone mentions a particular phrase (such as your company name) in a blog post, you get an RSS notification and can look and see what that person has said. This not only helps you get a sense of how users feel about your offerings, but also about what kind of language that blog's readers use for them. Later, we will show how to use free tools like Yahoo Pipes to monitor social media for common keyword-related activity.

Engaging with Web Visitors through More Targeted Search Referrals

Until now, we have focused on using keywords to attract a target audience to your content. But keywords are not the only parts of Web content that determine whether your content is relevant. A user can find the content on a page (with the same keywords) relevant one week and irrelevant the next. You might ask: How can that happen? If keyword usage determines relevance, how can attracting users to your pages though keywords drive users to information that they find irrelevant? Well, language is a lot more complex than creating a simple matching algorithm between keywords and users. If it were that simple, Web writing and editing would be a matter for technology and would not require human decisions. Fortunately, making good content decisions based on a variety of variables, including keyword usage, requires humans.

Suppose that a visitor to one of your pages has viewed all the information on it, but there have been no new updates since then. The content might still be relevant to the visitor's interests, but no longer relevant enough to reread. In a marketing context, users might come to your site one week to see what you are offering, and the next week to see how those offerings fit their needs. Once they are aware of your offerings, if you simply drive them back to the same page through search, you're creating an irrelevant experience—one that could end in a bounce and a bad user experience.

There are many more variables that affect relevance than we have space to list. Those are for linguists to determine, rather than writing instructors. But we can point you to one important variable beyond keywords that affects whether visitors will find the content on your pages relevant: *purpose*. If you tune your pages to the activities your users hope to accomplish when they arrive on your pages, you have a much better chance of getting them to engage with your content. *Engagement is* one way we measure relevance: If people click a link on your page, we can at least say that link is relevant to them. Sometimes engagement is merely a question of reading the content. Sometimes it's clicking a link. Sometimes it's getting users to comment or fill out a form. There are countless calls to action that a Web site can have—another key difference between print and Web. In print, you simply want to get your reader to read and comprehend your information. Perhaps you want the reader to be entertained or merely informed. However, you never want the reader to interact with a book—to write in the book in hopes that you will write back.

But on the Web, engagement or interaction is typically exactly what we want users to do. If all we want them to do is read and comprehend, we can provide PDFs for printing and reading offline. But good Web content is interactive. It compels the visitor to take action. So, in addition to tuning your page's content for keywords, you also must tune it for the interactive purpose of that page. The real trick is mapping the keyword phrase to the page's purpose. This isn't as hard as it might seem. It is merely a question of adding a verb to your keyword phrase that describes what you want users to do when they get to a particular page. For example, one page can have keyword phrases with *learn* in them, another page might have keyword phrases with *shop* in them.

The question is: How do we help users land on one of our pages that is relevant to a keyword and related to their purpose in seeking the information? We will attempt to give some answers to this question in this book. But a word of caution: There are very few general answers. Different environments demand different answers to complex search questions. You will never achieve perfect engagement levels; because of the complexity of Web interactions, some visitors will bounce. But we can give you a framework for answering the question, and improving your engagement rates with writing that is more focused on the purpose or user goal of the page.

Developing an Optimized Site Architecture

We think of print publications as mostly self-contained units. Sure, we refer to related works in the bibliography or source list of a publication. But we expect print publications to be consumed whole. This is another key difference between print and the Web. Web users do a lot more skimming and scanning than print users. Only after they determine that the information matches what they're looking for do they bother to read. This is a central insight of this book, and it affects every aspect of Web publishing, including design and architecture.

For our purposes, **Web architecture** is the practice of designing information experiences that help users find the information they're looking for. In a sense, writing for search engines is part of this practice. If you write in a way that helps users find information more easily through search engines than if they navigated to it from a home page, you are approaching an optimal user experience. But search is not enough, either; you also need to *design for navigation*. The goal is to create engagement, and in some cases, conversions. It's not enough to get a visitor to click a link; that click should land the user on a relevant page. Search can draw users to lower-level pages and encourage them to navigate up; or it can draw users to higher-level pages and enable them to navigate down. And horizontal navigation is also part of a good architectural plan. In any event, the content experience doesn't end with getting the user to come and click on something; you must get the user to engage with it.

Many architectural discussions at IBM and other companies focus on designing a hierarchy of pages that enables users to easily move from the top level to the specific information they're looking for. This is a good approach if you are designing a user experience for navigation. But it leaves out key considerations that can help users find information from search. Some search engines rely on **metadata**—extra-linguistic information hidden from view in the code of pages—to help determine the relevance of those pages. Though Google does not use metadata as part of its ranking, it does analyze how pages are interlinked with the rest of the Web to help determine relevance. Thus, architecting a set of pages for search engines necessarily includes paying attention to metadata and linking.

In this book, we focus on Google as the most popular search engine in the United States and elsewhere. From an architectural perspective, this means a thorough discussion of linking. This is the subject of an entire chapter later in the book.

Before we do that, we will first discuss how the standard practice of designing a hierarchy of related pages around a central topic or theme relates to keyword usage for search engines. To reach a more general audience, most architects design information around topics starting at a high level. This architecture should help users drill down into the information in the hierarchy, according to their individual needs. To enable this experience, you should choose different related keywords for each page in the topic, following the hierarchy. For example, on the IBM Web site, we might start with a high-level page on IBM Servers and then develop pages related to a specific product line, like the BladeCenter and other IBM offerings within this topic, such as BladeCenter hardware (Figure 1.1).

You might think this is a fairly straightforward process. The architect designs the hierarchy of pages, and the writer picks keywords to fit into it. We suggest that this process rarely works the way it is drawn up on paper. At IBM, we struggle with pages in a hierarchy that do not produce search referrals because users simply do not search on the keywords we chose for those pages. Imagine a hierarchy of pages in which the third level down the tree is

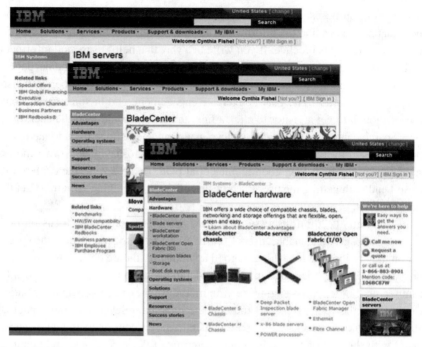

Figure 1.1   A hierarchy of pages in ibm.com.

the highest ranking page because it uses a popular keyword, yet the top-level page in this hierarchy gets little or no search engine traffic because few users ever search on its keyword.

We suggest (and will demonstrate later in the book) that the best practice is to optimize the top pages of the hierarchy with the most competitive keywords—the ones that draw the broadest audience. Pages lower in the hierarchy need to be optimized for narrower, more targeted audiences, who typically use long-tail keywords. You do this by choosing related keywords that are more likely to appeal to specific segments of the broader audience. The point of our chapter on the relationship between architecture and writing is that *architecture reflects writing practices:* When we create search-first architectures, we do a better job of creating an information experience for users for the whole hierarchy, not just for isolated pages within it.

The goal of information architecture is to serve users with relevant information. But how do you know what information is relevant to them? We suggest that the search-first architecture does a good job of creating relevant information for a large set of users, with less guesswork and less trial-and-error than common architecture processes. Keyword data is the best information available from which to design your information. It not only helps you isolate specific keywords that will draw higher volumes of users to specific pages, but it helps you understand how keywords and phrases are related to one another. If you optimize a hierarchy of pages for a set of related keywords, you not only direct users to specific pages they might be interested in; you can also get them to navigate to other pages in the hierarchy from their initial search referral. If they find the top-level pages relevant, chances are they will find pages targeted toward more narrow audiences even more relevant.

In large organizations with a complex matrix of Web sites, content creators can unwittingly compete for the same keywords, thus harming visitors' overall experience. For this reason, large organizations need to manage keywords across their whole site, not just within specific areas.

Suppose you own a part of a company's Web content—perhaps the marketing pages related to a portion of your company's product portfolio. You do all the keyword research related to that portfolio, develop a site architecture that maps pages to popular keywords and desired visitor interaction, and write optimized content for each page in the architecture. In short, you do everything right to attract the most targeted audience possible to your pages. However, suppose that a colleague owns the Web content for a related set of offerings in your company's portfolio. She does everything you do and optimizes her pages for the same keywords, all the way down to the long-tail ones. You are now unwittingly competing with your colleague for the same targeted audience.

As unlikely as this scenario is, competition is actually quite common in a company such as IBM that has a large and diverse portfolio of offerings, and many Web pages related to them. Even for themes such as Green IT, several efforts might spring up at the same time and could unwittingly compete with one another for the same users, unless these efforts are coordinated. For this reason, we recommend corporate-wide keyword management systems, which enable content owners to reserve specific keywords for specific pages. These systems can spread keyword usage across an enterprise in way that is similar to, but more pervasive than, what you do when you develop a keyword-based architecture around your theme or topic. With such a tool in place, you can optimize your enterprise for popular keywords and attract targeted audiences to the most important pages for your business.

Gaining Credibility through PageRank

As important as keyword usage is for your search efforts, it is less than half of the Google algorithm. The Google algorithm takes two primary things into account: **relevance,** which is a function of how keywords are used on a page; and **PageRank**, which is a function of how your page is interwoven into the Web's vast map of links. (There are other factors as well, such as the prominence of your site in the scheme of the Web, but those are beyond your influence as a Web writer. In this book, we will focus on keyword relevance and PageRank.) You can do everything right to improve the relevance of your pages by using keywords, yet still fail to get your page listed on the first page of Google results. If a particular keyword is highly competitive, meaning that lots of other sites are doing everything in their power to rank high for it, you will also need to improve your PageRank to get listed on that first page of Google, Bing, and other search engines.

For example, the keyword *Service Oriented Architecture,* or *SOA,* is highly competitive in Google—a lot of very smart companies spend a lot of money developing optimized pages around a cloud of keywords related to *SOA.* The only way to get on the first page of results in Google for *SOA* is to get credible pages around the Web to link to your SOA page. Google counts each link to your page as a vote of confidence for the content on your page. This is how Google overcomes the problem of relevance on the Web. Because the text alone cannot determine whether users will find the content relevant to them, and there are no better contextual cues to content than links, Google uses linking as its main contextual cue. All evidence indicates that Bing also uses links, and, if anything, gives them even greater weight than does Google.

As complicated as keyword usage can get, linking is much more complex. Search engines don't count every link to your pages as equally valuable. Some links get more **link juice,** or value, than others, depending on how valuable and relevant Google deems the site that links to your page.

We will explain some of this complexity later in the book. For now, suffice it to say that you need to develop a plan to promote your pages to high-value sites. Many sites have value simply because they serve as **link aggregators** related to a given topic. One example is Wikipedia: It contains relatively little original content, but it is an excellent place to begin researching a topic, because every source is a link to further research. (If you attempt to publish original content on Wikipedia in the sense that it lacks original sources, the content gets flagged as in need of support.) However, for technical reasons to be explained later, Wikipedia is not a great site from which to get link juice. It merely illustrates the point that sites like it, which link to deeper dives into research topics, are highly valued by users. And because users value them highly, search engines do as well. For this reason, these hubs of authority typically find themselves listed near the top of search results.

Our approach is to determine the best path to becoming a **hub of authority** on your topic. This requires a lot of deep thinking about the state of the art of your topic and a lot of research into the existing hubs of authority on it. How does your content fit into the matrix of authority on your topic? What contribution does your content make to the interlinked conversation related to your topic? How do you engage with other subject matter experts in your field to promote this contribution to the discussion? We will explore these and other questions to help you improve your PageRank in Google. And who knows, if you develop a good relationship with the recognized authorities in your field and your content makes a unique contribution to the field, you too can become a hub of authority and thus rank highly in search engines.

There are no shortcuts to becoming a hub of authority. To do so, you must gain the trust of other authorities for your topic. That takes time. Still, there are some tactics that can help you promote your content to authority sites. We will cover them in Chapter 8.

Capturing Social- and Rich-Media Opportunities

Print habits die hard. Chief among them is the habit of wanting to control the conversation. When you write for print, it's your tale and you control the telling—you control how the reader consumes the information. But when you write for the Web, the reader controls the pace and flow of information. Trying to control it is a surefire way to get users to bounce off your pages. The best you can do is to give users options they will want to choose. Part of gaining their trust to choose your content options—to click your links—is making it clear that it's their choice. Part of this is demonstrating that your content is not isolated, that it doesn't claim to have all the answers, and that it is but a small part of a bigger conversation.

The Web is an evolving medium, and users' expectations evolve with it. At this time, the fastest growing practice on the Web is sometimes called **social media.** Loosely defined, it is a set of practices that engage Web users to participate in the conversation rather than merely consume static information. These practices include blogs, wikis, forums, persona sites such as Facebook, microblogging sites such as Twitter, and the like. Social media is rapidly evolving to include graphics and video sharing and sophisticated syndication.

Nowhere is the Web more distinct from print publishing than in social media contexts. Users control the flow of information as they navigate through static Web pages; but they actually *contribute* to information in social media contexts. Here, their control of the information is complete. In extreme cases, users who make frequent comments on a blog are as important to the blog's success as its author. And a blog is not much more than an online opinion column if no one comments on its entries.

As the Web becomes more of a collaborative medium—more of a space for symposiums rather than lectures—users' expectations for the whole Web change. Even publishers of static Web content need to adjust their practices to engage users in conversations. Whether your site explicitly enables users to comment on its content or not, users expect it to. Social media has accelerated the need to give users more control over their information paths, even if your content is not intended to be shared and commented on.

For example, at one time IBM had a number of Web producers who preferred to get permission to republish content from other sources on their sites, rather than to link directly to the sources of that information. Fortunately, across the industry, this practice has long ago become a distant memory of how things used to be done in Web publishing. That memory is all that remains of writing habits that stem from print: "Let's keep users on our site.

Let's not let them leave." This attitude is self defeating on the Web. You lose users' trust when you try to control their experiences; and you lose potential PageRank, as well.

Because page rankings are a large part of Google's PageRank (and of Bing's similar algorithm) and are determined by how a community "votes" on the credibility of content, search is a social medium. Not surprisingly, improving your standing in the community by engaging users in social media contexts is a very effective way to gain credibility and PageRank. If you encourage users to pass your links, podcasts, and videos around to their friends, the PageRank for the pages on which those assets are accessed will grow virally. Since users expect this pass-along content to be ever more visual, search effectiveness is not just about text anymore. It is crucially about rich media as well.

The irony is that the more control you give users, the more they will want to visit your site. The more open you are in your reciprocal linking relationships to and from rich media on other sites, the more users will treat your site as a hub of authority and will keep coming back to hang out and explore new paths through your content. Later on, we will demonstrate in more detail how to take advantage of the social attitudes and habits of Web users.

This letting go of control of your information is a necessary, though sometimes painful, cultural shift in Web content practices. Because this shift is so necessary and fundamental to successful Web content efforts, we believe it deserves a chapter all its own.

Measuring Web Effectiveness

How do you know how well you are doing on Google? That is a rather easy question: You simply search on your keywords and see where your page ends up in the results. How do you know the volume of visitors you get from Google? This question is a little harder: You use a Web analytics tool such as Unica Netinsight to find out where your visitors are coming from and then filter the results to show only those who come from Google. You can also run reports in modern Web analytics tools that show what keywords brought users to your pages, and in what volume.

The more detailed you want to get in understanding the effectiveness of your search efforts, the harder the questions become. You can get a lot of information related to data such as Google ranking, Google referrals, raw traffic, no-results keywords, click throughs, and customer feedback specific to search, but correlating that data is quite difficult. The goal of this kind of research is to measure engagement: How many users are doing the things you want them to do on a page, such as downloading a white paper, filling a survey, taking a poll, or making a comment? We will discuss a best practice in gathering and correlating the various search effectiveness later in the book.

For the purpose of this discussion, suffice it here to say that how you define and measure search effectiveness is a fundamental facet of using search to target audiences with content. Search efforts rarely work exactly as they were drawn up on paper. More often than not, you will find aspects of your search efforts that underperform expectations. In these cases, you will have to go back to your pages and fine-tune your content to better target your desired audience. If you find a high bounce rate, for example, you might need to change the language on the page to develop better engagement with your target audience. The practices outlined above and detailed later in this book can help you do a better job of search optimization when you first develop and publish content. But language on the Web is a complex medium, and you can expect to have to do a certain amount of reworking to achieve better engagement. For this reason, measurement is a critical phase in search optimization work.

Also, to compete for users, search engines are evolving rapidly. If an engine changes after you publish information, it might make sense to go back and tweak your pages in ways that can help you rank better for it. To do this, you need analytics tools and best practices. We will describe how to use available Web analytics tools to measure search effectiveness and develop action items to improve existing content in the process.

How the Web Medium Has Evolved from Its Oral and Print Origins

On Media Determinism

Imagine if the only way to learn anything was to memorize an entire story based on a series of tone poems. Prior to literacy, that is how all knowledge was transmitted from one person to another. Consider the Homeric epic poems. The whole of the *Iliad* and the *Odyssey* are written like a series of tone poems to be sung. And that is how they were relayed for centuries before they were finally written down. With no text to rely on, there is no way one can remember what occupies thousands of pages of writing without the poetic structure of the stories (mnemonics). Lacking text, preliterate cultures developed elaborate mnemonic devices and embedded them into their storytelling. Because these mnemonic devices occupied so much of their minds, they did not have space for other kinds of thinking. The study of how the medium (such as oral, print, or Web) that you use affects what you can and can't think about or communicate is called *media determinism*.[1]

Media determinism is the primary lens that we use in this book to study the differences between writing for print and writing for the Web. Most of this lens was developed by Marshall McLuhan and Walter Ong to study how human thinking evolved as our cultures evolved from oral to print. We extend this lens to look at how human thinking is changing as we move from print culture to Web culture. But before we talk about the evolution from print to Web, it is useful to consider the evolution from oral to print, if for no other reason than to engage the skeptical reader in examples of how the medium we use affects our thinking. When the reader is ready to accept the lens of media determinism, we can use this lens to view the transformation from print to Web.

---

1. Marshall McLuhan is famous for saying, "The medium is the message" (or massage). Roughly, what he means is that the medium one uses to communicate determines what one can communicate. McLuhan and his student Walter Ong pioneered a kind of language analysis that powerfully explains how human language works differently depending on the medium. McLuhan and Ong focused on the distinctive qualities of literate cultures to understand how literacy changes the way we think and communicate. They used sophisticated cultural and historical analysis to demonstrate that when a culture becomes literate, the nature of its stories changes.

There are countless ways in which a literate culture differs from a preliterate one. One very important difference is in the way the human brain works. If there is no longer a need to remember all the names and places and things people have done because they are written down, the mind is free to think in different ways. One important facet of literate culture is abstract thought. Instead of *particular* people, places and things, humans are free to think about *kinds* of people, places and things, and to develop classification systems and every manner of logic relating kinds of things. Philosophy, science, and mathematics require the signs and symbols of the written word. If you've ever tried to work out a complex math problem in your head, you understand the importance of symbols in the development of human thought.

It is tempting to see the transition from oral cultures to literate cultures as a matter of absolutes, as though one moment people thought in oral ways and the next moment they thought in literate ways. In fact, the transition is much more gradual. Literacy is not easily acquired by a culture. In western cultures, the transition from an oral culture to a literate one took place over thousands of years. Even in the twenty-first century, remnants of orality persist in a primarily literate culture. The popularity of lyricists such as Bob Dylan speaks to remnants of how humans' brains were once wired, if nothing else, to augment our primarily literate understanding. Even today, print doesn't supplant oral traditions; it augments them. With multiple choices of how to communicate, we can tailor our medium to fit the circumstance.

As our print culture becomes ever more a Web culture, we need to look at the differences between print and Web communication with a similar lens, just as we view the transition from oral culture to print culture. The similarities are striking.

- The move from oral to print was gradual, as is the move from print to Web. Web publishing has not replaced, and will not replace, the need for print. It merely augments print and provides a means for quicker information retrieval, among other things.

- The move from oral to print changed the way humans think, as does the move from print to Web. Consider the change in our thinking as we consume ever more numerous, smaller bits of information, made possible by Web applications such as Twitter.

- The move from oral to print had wide-reaching socio-economic implications, as does the move from print to Web. The printing press brought literacy to the masses for a narrow band of learning; the Web brings literacy to the masses for a much broader scope of human knowledge.

Showing these and other facets of the evolution of human media is a project for a whole academic discipline—not for this book. Our intent is not to delve too deeply into this discipline. But neither can we ignore its insights. What we provide instead is a small corner of the vast literature on the subject, one which is particularly illuminating in showing how media evolution affects the way we think and write.

Along the way, we will develop a view of Web writing effectiveness that isn't just a how-to book on writing, but that helps you understand why our approach works.

Spaces between Words

The change from oral to literate culture in western societies was gradual, but not uniform. Some moments in this history created great earthquakes of change in human thought, and others, mere tremors. Of all the milestones in the transition from oral to print, one event in western history perhaps best helps us understand media distinctions and transitions: the invention of spaces between words. Other events were important, of course, but we focus on this one because it contains many of the features that we want to highlight in the move from print to Web.

Prior to the Scholastic period (beginning in the twelfth century A.D.), most texts contained no spaces between words. It is hard for modern literate people to understand what reading was like before there were spaces between words. Imagine looking at a line in which all the words flow together, and consider how difficult it was to read line after line of text printed in script. The only way to make sense of it was to read it aloud; if you tried to read it silently, you frequently made mistakes in slicing up lines of text into discrete words (see the sidebar explaining how the eyes cue into spaces between words to read text).

What Reading Was Like before Spaces between Words

Consider the following sentence:

Readabletextrequiresspacesinoredertounderstandwhereonewordendsan-danotherbegins.

If you read it silently, this is utter nonsense. But try reading it aloud. It still is tough, in part because it is a lot for your mind to process and parse. But if you read it aloud a couple of times, you should be able to parse it correctly:

Readable text requires spaces in order to understand where one word ends and another begins.

Now try this paragraph:

thesummer'sgoneandalltheflowersaredying
'tisyou'tisyoumustgoandimustbide
butcomeyebackwhensummer'sinthemeadow
orwhenthevalley'shushedandwhitewithsnow
'tisi'llbehereinsunshineorinshadow
ohdannyboyohdannyboyiloveyouso

Even with all lower-case letters, these lines from an old folk song can be more easily parsed (and notice that it gets easier as you go along), because the lyric has

continues

rhyming and meter that help your mind keep track of where you are. If writers wanted to be understood (which was not always a given in preliterate times), they wrote poetically. And readers would read aloud, muttering line after line in order to grasp the meaning of the texts, which looked like this passage from Cicero's *De finibus bonorum et malorum* (Figure 2.1).

NEQVEPORROQVISQVAMESTQVIDOLOREMIPSVMQVI
ADOLORSITAMETCONSECTETVRADIPISCIVELIT

Figure 2.1   An excerpt from Cicero's *De finibus bonarum et malorum*, which in modern punctuation is: Neque porro quisquam est qui dolorem ipsum quia dolor sit amet, consectetur, adipisci uelit.

Because pre-Scholastic texts were read aloud, writers used the same mnemonic techniques that oral cultures use for their mythologies—meter, rhythm, and so forth. The primary value for the written word in those days was the lack of a need to remember *Iliad*–length oral passages. But the reader still needed to remember passages as long as a page in length before actually grasping the sense of the text. Consequently, readers' thought patterns still had an oral character to them.

It was monks in the scriptorium who started inserting spaces between words. They did this for copying. It was a lot easier to copy text with spaces than without. The practice began in the ninth century in Ireland and spread across Europe over the next three centuries. Not until the twelfth century did the practice of uniform spacing become the standard across Europe. Though originally devised to ease copying, it soon had widespread effects on the way people read and understood content, and on how writers tailored their manuscripts for the reader.

Paul Saenger (1997) wrote the definitive work exploring the effects of spaces between words in the context of how the medium changed the message. He noted that

Whereas the ancient reader had relied on aural memory to retain an ambiguous series of sounds as a preliminary stage to extracting meaning, the scholastic reader swiftly converted signs to words, and groups of words to meaning, after which both the specific words and their order might quickly be forgotten. Memory in reading was primarily employed to retain the general sense of the clause, the sentence and the paragraph. Albertus Magnus, Thomas Aquinas, Roger Bacon, Duns Scotus, and William of Ockham, despite their divergent national origins, all wrote similar scholastic Latin remarkable for its clarity and precision of expression, which was achieved at the sacrifice of classical rhythm, meter, and mellifluous sonority. (Saenger 1997, 254–5)

The effects of using spaces between words were far reaching. By the thirteenth century, literacy and original writing blossomed, even before the printing press. Writing soon became a medium that enabled all kinds of expression not seen since the Greeks, such as grammar, logic, theoretical mathematics, and science (Saenger 1997, 202–5).

One important effect was the notion that it was now the scribe's responsibility to make the text readable for the audience. Before then, literacy was an elitist activity that took years of leisure to acquire. It was a mark of this learning, and of breeding, if one could read text *inscriptura continua* (without spaces). It was therefore not the responsibility of the scribe to make the text clear; the scribe wrote as he or she deemed fit. If readers managed to decipher the text, they were worthy of its contents. As more and more writing became accessible, readers began demanding clarity, and writers who did not write with the reader in mind fell out of favor and out of our literary histories.

Another effect of using spaces between words related to the way libraries were set up. Prior to silent reading, libraries were constructed with carrels that kept the muttering of the scribe to a dull roar. Book and scroll retrieval were the purview of the librarian. And indexes at the back of books were nonexistent. But the construction of Scholastic libraries is much like the libraries of today, with open collections and central tables where readers can sit side by side without disturbing each other. Most books in these libraries contained back-of-the-book indexes. These libraries also included the first catalogues, "with alphabetical author indexes and special union catalogues representing the holdings of libraries in a city or region" (Saenger 1997, 263). For the first time, literacy included not just being able to decipher an individual text, but understanding the text in the context of a genre or collection. It is no surprise that the first modern universities were founded during the Scholastic period.

The invention of spaces between words was only one point in a string of developments that contributed to the maturing of the print medium. Because clarity became a value of writing with spaces, spaces between words opened literacy for the masses to understand. This ultimately ushered in the Renaissance (Eisenstein 1983). But the Renaissance was only truly made possible by the invention of the printing press. Parchment and vellum were expensive. Copyists were limited mostly to monasteries, and to private publishers, who charged a king's ransom for a book. There was no practical way to get books to the masses until the printing press and the complementary Chinese invention of paper—which was as cheap as papyrus and as durable as parchment. Libraries rapidly expanded their collections. Publishers could produce books in enough quantity to drive the price per book down to a level affordable to the expanding merchant middle class. And institutions of higher learning began springing up everywhere, where middle class youth could gain their letters. These universities became the centers of new knowledge, organized by discipline—much as today's universities are.

We won't delve into all the effects of the printing press. Consult McLuhan and Eisenstein if you're interested in those topics. But we do want to highlight how the printing press, together with such inventions as spaces between words, changed the reader/writer relationship. Prior to print becoming a mass medium, the practice of audience analysis was a lost ancient art (specifically, Aristotelian art). Scholastic readers had quite similar learning backgrounds in the scriptorium. The production of secular books was confined to the trades, which likewise had clear learning curricula. All learning was conducted in Latin, which was universally understood in Europe among learned people. So writing for the medieval reader did not require much audience analysis. One wrote on topics of interest, free from worrying about the reader, aside from conventional notions of clarity and grammar, which were relatively new at that time.

As print has evolved since medieval times, audience analysis has ebbed and flowed with the changing reader/writer relationship. Print became ever more a mass medium, spanning languages and cultures, incorporating many purposes outside of the practical sciences (such as literature), and branching out into other forms, such as newspapers and magazines. And effective writing evolved with it (Figure 2.2).

Outside of literary art, writing for print as we encounter it today is first and foremost about understanding the discrete audience for which the publication is produced, and writing for that audience. Of course, you never really know your audience, which is a convenient fiction (Ong 1984, 177). But the fiction is based on facts or stereotypes about the readers of the publication. So writing for print must start with at least trying to understand your audience, and either addressing your writing to their known attitudes or invoking the audience to follow your prescribed path through a topic in the absence of such knowledge. Except in specialized circumstances, you really know very little about your actual print audience. That's why writing for print often concerns itself with expressing interesting things in interesting ways and hoping your audience connects with it.

The point of this brief history of the print medium is to convince you that our communication is often affected by the medium we use. Some of the changes in the print medium—such as the invention of spaces between words—began as conveniences to save time or resources. But they had profound unintended effects on the way the print medium was used to communicate thereafter. These changed not only the practice of writing, but also the topics that writers explored, and the very way readers thought about those topics. The rest of this chapter, and the rest of the book, will delve into similar evolutions in the Web medium,

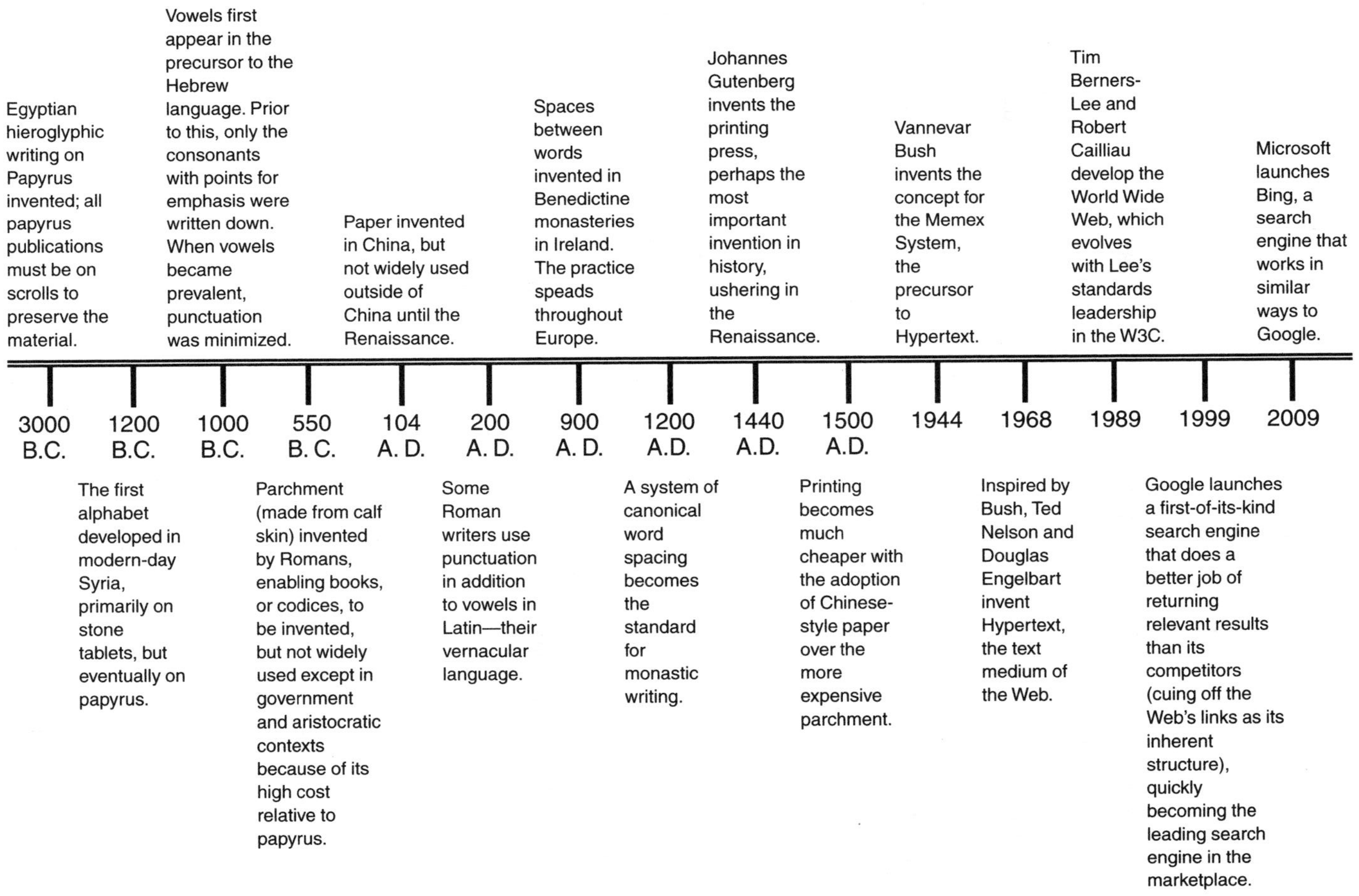

Figure 2.2 A timeline of media determinism.

3000 B.C.	Egyptian hieroglyphic writing on Papyrus invented; all papyrus publications must be on scrolls to preserve the material.
1200 B.C.	The first alphabet developed in modern-day Syria, primarily on stone tablets, but eventually on papyrus.
1000 B.C.	Vowels first appear in the precursor to the Hebrew language. Prior to this, only the consonants with points for emphasis were written down. When vowels became prevalent, punctuation was minimized.
550 B.C.	Parchment (made from calf skin) invented by Romans, enabling books, or codices, to be invented, but not widely used except in government and aristocratic contexts because of its high cost relative to papyrus.
104 A.D.	Paper invented in China, but not widely used outside of China until the Renaissance.
200 A.D.	Some Roman writers use punctuation in addition to vowels in Latin—their vernacular language.
900 A.D.	Spaces between words invented in Benedictine monasteries in Ireland. The practice speads throughout Europe.
1200 A.D.	A system of canonical word spacing becomes the standard for monastic writing.
1440 A.D.	Johannes Gutenberg invents the printing press, perhaps the most important invention in history, ushering in the Renaissance.
1500 A.D.	Printing becomes much cheaper with the adoption of Chinese-style paper over the more expensive parchment.
1944	Vannevar Bush invents the concept for the Memex System, the precursor to Hypertext.
1968	Inspired by Bush, Ted Nelson and Douglas Engelbart invent Hypertext, the text medium of the Web.
1989	Tim Berners-Lee and Robert Cailliau develop the World Wide Web, which evolves with Lee's standards leadership in the W3C.
1999	Google launches a first-of-its-kind search engine that does a better job of returning relevant results than its competitors (cuing off the Web's links as its inherent structure), quickly becoming the leading search engine in the marketplace.
2009	Microsoft launches Bing, a search engine that works in similar ways to Google.

which were perhaps developed as conveniences, but which are beginning to have profound effects on our communication, and on the topics we are able to communicate. In particular, how we write relevant content for a Web audience is as revolutionary as how writers needed to write for a print audience after the invention of spaces between words.

The Limits of Print Media and the Origins of the Web

Though print literacy opened the mind to new ways of thinking, it too is limited. Walk into a library and you will soon be overwhelmed by the amount of knowledge contained on its shelves. There is only enough time to consume a tiny portion of that knowledge. As the centuries of scholarship have advanced since the Scholastic period, the scope of what one can master has continuously shrunk. By the middle of the twentieth century, the advancement of new knowledge had become so specialized that people within related fields often couldn't communicate effectively with one another.

In this environment, writing also became a relatively specialized task. Outside of the mass media, each periodical had a well-understood audience and purpose. An aspiring writer for one of these periodicals simply needed to read it long enough to understand the gaps in research and fill those gaps with prose that fit that periodical's guidelines. Audience analysis was also relatively easy—the readers were the other authors who frequently published in the journal. If you had read an academic periodical long enough, you could form a good understanding of the audience based on the writers who published in it. But if you attempted to publish in a journal for a related field, you might have more trouble succeeding. It was as though each specialized journal had its own way of communicating in print. This stifled innovation, which needed good communication between practitioners in related fields.

In 1945, a visionary MIT professor named Vannevar Bush published an influential article in the *Atlantic Monthly*—"As We May Think" (1945)—proposing a way for science to transcend the limitations of print. Bush saw clearly the need for a radical new information system that could give researchers access to the work of colleagues in a fraction of the time and space required by the antiquated print journal. "There is a growing mountain of research," Bush wrote. "But there is increased evidence that we are being bogged down as specialization extends. The investigator is staggered by the findings and conclusions of thousands of other workers—conclusions which he cannot find time to grasp, much less to remember, as they appear" (Bush 1945, 1–2). However, Bush's proposed Memex system relied on antiquated technology, which had various limitations of time and space.[2] So his vision was never realized in his lifetime. (He died in 1974.)

---

2. One such antiquated technology Bush refers to is stenotype, which provides a written record of speech. But speech is not an expressive medium for such things as conceptual, mathematical, or scientific findings, as McLuhan, Ong, and others pointed out repeatedly in the decades after Bush.

It was not until computers became reliable and economical tools with which to store and communicate information that hypertext was born. Ted Nelson and Douglas Engelbart credit Bush's essay with the genesis of the idea for hypertext. And it wasn't until various hypertext collections were connected by the Internet that the basic concepts of the Memex system began to take shape in the form of the World Wide Web.

The Web was developed by Tim Berners-Lee and Robert Cailliau in 1989 for a group of physicists associated with CERN in Geneva, Switzerland (Berners-Lee and Fischetti 1999). The idea was quite simple: provide a way to publish hypertext over the Internet collaboratively. The original purpose of the Web was to link communities of physicists in order to publish their work more quickly and efficiently than the static print journals could do. Berners-Lee's original browser concept resembled current-day wikis more than Web pages, in the sense that the reader could edit and amend text just as much as passively read it. But that concept was replaced by a more secure Web experience because of the phenomena of hacking and online vandalism.

The reason for the Web's success had already been summed up by Bush 44 years earlier in the *Atlantic Monthly*. He realized that in print, specialists published findings that interlaced, but without the connections ever being made. To use Bush's words, "The means we use for threading through the maze to the momentarily important item is the same as was used in the days of the square-rigged ship" (Bush 1945, 2). Science had outgrown this mode of information sharing, and physicists were the first scientists to experiment with a new medium to meet their needs.

Because CERN was the largest Internet node in Europe, the Web became a global phenomenon in a few short years. It quickly burst out of its physics confines and into every academic discipline. Within five years of its widespread use in academia, corporations saw the vast potential of the new medium and began making commercial use of the Web. What followed was a series of refinements and standards efforts that enabled Web publishers to create vast searchable repositories of content on every imaginable subject. It also evolved beyond an immense interlinked library of hypertext to become a commerce engine and an agent of organizational and social change. Just as print evolved over the centuries, the Web continues to evolve to better meet the needs of information retrieval and sharing.

Print Content versus Web Content

We are in the midst of an accelerated version of the move from oral to print culture. In this case, we are moving from a static print culture to a dynamic Web culture. This new shift is changing the way we think. But because we are in the middle of it, we have a hard time objectively analyzing just how our thinking is changing. Also, it is a bit of a moving target: As Web change accelerates, it's tough to encapsulate the whole of Web practice into a static medium such as this book. For that reason, we don't seek to exhaustively show the differences between Web media and print media. Rather, we will focus on the salient features that contribute to the kind of seismic change like that of the invention of spaces between words—the sheer quantity of unstructured content at the fingertips of anyone who uses the Web.

The key facets of the Web that differ from print are as follows.

- Because the Web is so vast and complex, Web users scan content to determine relevance. They only read after they're sure the content is relevant to them.

- Readers only determine that a page is relevant to them if it matches their use of the words on the page. If you use technical or figurative language that differs from audience expectations, they are likely to ignore your work, rather than reading it.

- Because users can land on a page from any number of starting points, especially search engines, you can't assume that your audience has the background needed to understand your content. In a sense, it's not your story, it's the user's.

- Because the Web includes a lot of bad information, Web readers are more skeptical than print readers. If you get users to read your content, you must provide clear evidence for it—preferably in the form of links to authorities on the topic.

- Web writing is not permanent. You could say it's never finished. Because it's relatively easy to update Web pages, Web users expect pages to do this regularly. And the Web medium gives the writer the ability to test how a page is performing and make adjustments to better target the audience.

There are many more differences between writing for print and writing for the Web. We will limit the discussion for the present purposes to these five salient differences.

Basic Information Retrieval on the Web

The most important cultural practice on the Web is that of *scanning*. Print readers have a relatively easy time finding the information they need. They can go to the library, which is organized in a very rigorous way to help them find information. Books are organized by genre, author, and title. Libraries have codes such as the Dewey Decimal System to help users find the exact match for the books they're looking for. And they have computerized card catalogs, which are now nearly as sophisticated as search engines, to help them. So when readers find the books or periodicals they are looking for, they can begin reading confidently, without worrying about whether those items are relevant to their needs.

The main difference between a library and the Web is the lack of a standard organizational system for information on the Web. Numerous such systems have been tried, but none have become pervasive. The Web is like a library where everything is organized by publisher, and there are millions of publishers, who each produce information of all sorts. This is a vastly more complex universe than a library. Users typically find information using search engines on the Web, but unlike with a library card catalog, they can't assume that the results of the search are relevant to them. Because the snippets of information that search engines display are so meager, users often must click through to the results to determine relevance. A large percentage of users won't read a page's contents until they scan it and determine that it is indeed relevant to their needs.

Because the Web is so vast and seemingly disorganized, Web users don't often waste time reading. Suppose that a user enters a few key words into a search engine and gets pages upon pages of results. How does he or she decide what to read first? Typically, Web readers click results near the top of the first page of the search results, scan the pages to determine if they are relevant to them, and only after making that determination do they actually read. If a page doesn't seem relevant within a few seconds, they click the **Back** button, or "bounce" off the page, back to the search results, and try another page. After bouncing off of three or four pages, readers become frustrated and will then refine their search strings to better match what is relevant to them. Jakob Nielsen (June 2008) shows that most Web users behave this way. There are outliers, but the common understanding is that you as a Web author have on average 3 to 6 seconds of scanning to demonstrate your page's relevance to a user.

So the question is: How do you write for audiences that only give you a few seconds to determine if you're worth their time? The answer to this question depends on the answer to another one: How does a Web audience determine the relevance of a page through scanning? We will cover that question in Chapter 3, which deals with how relevance is determined on the Web. But in order to answer the question about relevance, we must first understand features of the Web medium that differ from the print medium. Savvy Web users take advantage of these subtle features of the Web medium to help them determine relevance.

Meaning as Use on the Web

In print, writers typically define their terms up front, and use those definitions throughout a text or group of texts. In the common usage this is a matter of either using a conventional definition, or of modifying one to fit the need. These terms must fall within an acceptable range of language use in order to make sense. But print writers have control over how they use and define their terms, and they often use technical definitions for the sake of clarity. Readers must cede this control if they wish to continue making sense of what they read.

On the Web, the roles are reversed. Readers determine what *they think* a word or term means, and writers need to pay attention to this first and foremost. The writer is best served by keeping these conventional or community definitions in mind, because users will use them in their searches. Readers will tell you if your use of language deviates too much from the community usage. How? If you use terms for which users search in an unusual way, they will not find your pages relevant to them. And in many searches, they will find pages that clearly are *not* relevant. An obvious example is a search on "orange." Novice users who search on such a generic term might get results for the fruit or the pigment. If they are shopping for orange paint, they will not find pages related to the fruit relevant to them. Or if the relevance is not clear from the snippet in the search result, users might click through to the wrong page. When this happens, they typically bounce back to the search results page and refine their search to something more promising, like "orange paint."

Suppose that you use a term on a Web page in a way that deviates from its conventional use, in terms of search results. And suppose that you also do everything necessary to make your page rank highly for search engines when users search for that term, or keyword. Users will find your content; but they will fairly quickly find that it is irrelevant to them—they were looking for information related to the conventional use of the term. Thus, they will bounce back to the results page and never return.

Another likely scenario if you use a term unconventionally is that your page will not rank highly for that term in the first place, because the search engine algorithm will determine that it is not relevant to users searching on it. This will practically guarantee low traffic for your page. When you write for the Web, it is best to learn how your target audience uses terms and adopt their usage, rather than trying to coin terms or create technical definitions for common terms.

One way that print writers often try to make their writing interesting is to use clever puns and double meanings to spice up the language, especially in headlines. This might make for a more interesting read, especially in magazines and newspapers, but it will not help you reach your target audience. For example, an ESPN.com headline read, "Closing The Book." The story was about the Cleveland Indians signing "closer" (a "relief pitcher" who pitches the last inning or two and "closes out" a baseball game) Kerry Wood to a free agent contract. Users searching for information on this story would not likely use the term "book" in their search queries; hence, searches might not find that story. Though the pun may make the writing more interesting, it defeats the purpose of having a story on the Web in the first place. This is one case where common print practices, such as using puns, do not translate well to the Web. It is better to have a lot of targeted traffic to pages that seem less interesting to the writer, than to have very little traffic to pages that might seem more interesting to him or her. Writing for the Web isn't about *what's clever or interesting to the writer*; it's about *what's relevant to the reader.* At least that's the position that we take in this book.

Writing for Skeptical Web Readers

In part because there are almost as many publishers as readers on the Web (in the age of blogs and social networking sites), readers do not have the traditional sense of trust that they place in print media. Unless you happen to work for one of the few trusted sources on the Web, your Web writing must assume that the reader has to be convinced. It is not enough to simply state claims; you must also prove them. But since you have only a few seconds to demonstrate your trustworthiness to a reader who is scanning a Web page, your proof cannot be complicated. You can show your trustworthiness in other ways, though, such as by providing links to many complimentary resources, using short, punchy descriptive phrases. They themselves cannot prove your points, though; the resources must do this. But if you provide a nonthreatening environment that entices users to open the resources that show your site's authority, you have a better chance of success than if you overwhelm them by trying to prove that authority before they're ready.

Unlike with print, Web credibility must be earned. It takes time to develop regular visitors who trust you. And there are no shortcuts to credibility. But you can increase your chances by getting highly ranked by Google (or Bing) on your topic, which will draw users to your site. Because Google's search results have credibility for users, they will likely give you the benefit of the doubt if they come to your site from Google. In keeping with this book's theme, closing any credibility gap for your Web site is as much about writing for search engines as it is about writing for your audience.

Another approach that we highlight in this book deals with social media. Credibility on the Web is not assigned by individuals, but by entire communities of like-minded users. Getting these users to find and share your content with each other is the ultimate way to gain credibility on the Web. It starts with search optimization, but it continues with social media tactics that you can use to deepen your relationship with loyal readers. The ultimate goal is to become a **hub of authority**, so that credible members of your community will link to your pages from their sites. This not only enhances your credibility in the community, but it is perhaps the most effective way to improve your search ranking, especially for topics with a lot of competition. Having Web credibility takes time and effort, but if you follow the practices we outline in this book, you will get there eventually.

The Perpetually Unfinished Web Page

We mentioned earlier that the Web medium gives you an opportunity to understand your audience in ways you never can with print. Writing a book can seem like sending out a message in a bottle. You never know who will pick it up, read it, quote from it, and share it with colleagues. This forces print writers to form convenient fictions about who their audience is and how they will make use of the book. It also forces print writers to interest their audiences with elaborate literary devices that compel them to continue reading and follow the static information flow.

On the Web, you may not know who your audience is, but you *can* know how they use your information. Web metrics tools can tell you where your users came from, how long they spent on your pages, whether or not they bounced off them, and the paths they took through your pages if they stayed. If your users came from Google, you can also know what words and phrases they used to get to your pages. And if you let users make comments on your writing, you can get direct feedback.

Because it is easy to update an existing Web page, it is a common practice for Web publishers to adjust pages based on the information they get from these metrics tools. If a particular link is popular, perhaps you want to draw more attention to it. If another link is not at all popular, perhaps you want to find a different source to support your points. If users tell you they don't like something, you can change it and thank them for the feedback. This kind of direct engagement with the audience allows Web writers to address them as real individuals rather than seeing them as convenient fictions.

Because Web publishers can treat their Web pages as dynamic, living documents that address their audiences better as time goes on, more and more Web users expect them to do this. Web audiences frown on stale content, and they will tell you this by not clicking on links and by bouncing if your content doesn't interest them anymore. In those cases, it is your job to either update the content or take it down. Some sites provide archives to enable researchers to find bookmarked information. But your active pages can and should be tested and adjusted regularly.

Summary

We cannot emphasize strongly enough how different Web writing is from print writing. And as the Web evolves into an ever more social medium, writing for the Web is becoming as different from writing for print as writing in one language differs from writing in another. Translation from English into, say, German requires not only translating the words, but also transliteration into the culture of the German-speaking people in the target audience. In the same way, attempting to translate print writing into the Web medium requires a kind of transliteration into the culture of the Web users. For this reason, it is typically better to just write for the Web in the first place in order to appeal to the practices of Web readers. This chapter is a survey of the prevalent cultural practices of Web readers.

In a sense, the Web is a victim of its own success. Because it is relatively cheap and easy to publish information on it, writers for the Web must deal with several issues not yet seen in the print world.

- **Web content is unstructured.** The content itself must provide the structure. Because of this, Web users don't read Web pages until they first discern whether the content is relevant to their needs. This differs from print content in the sense that the print world has many conventional ways of structuring publications, such as by author, by genre, or through the Dewey Decimal System. It is much less likely that readers will access an irrelevant publication from this structured system than that they will access an irrelevant Web page from a simple Web search.

- **Meaning on the Web is determined by the reader rather than the writer.** Because so many terms and expressions have multiple meanings, Web readers must first determine if the use of a term or expression on a page matches their expectation before deciding whether to read the content on that page or look for another page. This differs from print in the sense that authors of print publications can use their terms as they choose, while readers are required to conform their understanding to the authors' meaning, within reason.

- **On the Web, the writer is not in control of the story; the user is.** Because the Web allows for all kinds of navigation paths determined by the user, the "story" could be a collection of content from multiple sources, authors and contexts. This differs from print media, in which the writer tells a story and leads the audience to follow that story, or information path. As a Web writer, you can't assume that readers followed your prescribed navigation path to get to your content. For example, they might have landed directly on a given page from a search engine. So you must break information into small chunks and give users many ways to navigate to the ones that are relevant to them. And you cannot assume that your reader knows the contextual background information for a content module.

- Because results can be published quickly on it, **the Web does not have the levels of quality control that print media typically have.** For this reason, Web journals have not replaced print journals altogether in academia. And print will always occupy an important role for more permanent information. The editorial review of print journals tends to give them more credibility than publications created only for the Web. This means that Web users tend to be more skeptical than print users, although this is evolving as Web content governance evolves. But at the time of writing, most Web audiences do tend to be skeptical.

- **Web writing is never finished.** The writer gets the information to a certain minimum standard of quality, posts it, and begins watching the audience interact with it. Based on this interaction, the writer is expected to edit and update the content to better serve the audience.

These facts about the Web medium fundamentally change the reader/writer relationship and the concept of audience analysis at the heart of that relationship. Writing for Web readers requires surrendering control of the story and giving readers easy, clear paths to the information they seek. But it is not devoid of audience analysis. On the contrary, the Web lets writers tailor their content to the audience based on how the audience interacts with it. Even before publishing, Web writers can form a fairly accurate understanding of the word usage habits of their expected readers, based on information mined from search engine and social media usage. This book is about using that enhanced audience knowledge, which only the Web can provide, to create relevant content for your audience.

Writing Relevant Content for the Web Audience

Knowing what you know about how Web users find, scan, and ultimately use Web content, how do you create relevant content for your target audience on the Web? That is the question we will begin to answer in this chapter. The complete answer to this question is the subject of a whole book. And even then, there is no formula for every challenge you will face in connecting with your target audience. But we can lay a conceptual framework to help you make intelligent Web content decisions. We begin laying that framework in this chapter.

Providing relevance for your target audience fuels your writing. It determines what you write, how you write, and how you design Web content to cue into Web users' needs. Relevance is the coin of the Web realm, and that is not in much dispute. But despite the general understanding of this point, the practice of creating relevant Web content leaves much to be desired. Why? The main reason is that the medium is relatively new and continually evolving. Many site owners assume that there is not much difference between writing for print and writing for the Web. So they apply the same processes for the Web that they do for print publications. But the practice of writing for the Web is so different from print writing that their content is often not relevant to the users who find it, if users find it at all.

Suppose you assume, like so many content owners, that writing for the Web is similar to print in many ways. You develop a topic structure and flow not unlike the chapters of a book. You consider how users might follow your flow sequentially from topic to topic. And based on this topic flow, you assume that users know topics at higher levels of the topic structure if they are on topics at lower levels. In short, your content planning resembles planning book chapters, except that you might allow users to skip topic pages they are already familiar with. According to this scheme, if users find your home page relevant, they should also find the related pages relevant.

This is not a bad practice in and of itself, but it ignores the most important aspect of Web publishing. Namely, it does not take into account users who come to your pages from other sites, especially search engines. If other site owners find your content useful (your sincerest hope), they will link to it. And they won't necessarily link to the top page of a topic hierarchy, or to your site map (the Web equivalent of a table of contents). More often than not, they will link to lower-level pages in your site—those that are most directly relevant to the points they are trying to make. In the case of search engines, they will link to the pages that are the most relevant to the keywords that users enter into search fields. The results will be based more on the semantics of your pages than on where your pages are located within your site architecture.

We suggest that you should assume that most of your users come to your pages from search engines. If they navigate to one of your pages from others in your environment, you know that the links they click will lead them to relevant experiences, because you control those information paths. Consider that challenge solved. But if you can develop relevant content for users who come to your pages from external sites, especially search engines, you can dramatically increase the overall relevance of your content for your visitors. Search use has increased fairly steadily since Google launched in 1999. It will never entirely replace navigation, and other kinds of external referrals will always be present. But developing relevant content for the search audience will do more to improve the overall relevance of your content than any other Web writing or site architecture practice.

Who Is Your Web Audience?

In print contexts, the writer controls how content is conveyed. If readers want to understand print writing, they must follow the flow of information that the writer presents. You might not want to read the words in this chapter, but if you want to understand the rest of the book, you need to do so. As book writers, we have the luxury of presenting information in the way we think is best. Though we want to be sensitive to the audience, we honestly don't know them, and therefore, we mostly write the way we think is best and hope they understand us.

In particular, some of the information we present here might be irrelevant to our audience (you), either because you already know it or you just want to skip past the conceptual stuff and get to the how-to part of this book. We know you're interested in writing, so you will be inclined to give us the benefit of the doubt if the information is relevant to that. But we don't know your time constraints, patience level, or existing knowledge. So we present the information that we think will serve most of our readers in the best way we know how, and hope you will cut us some slack if we don't address your needs perfectly.

If this were a Web text, we could present the information in a more modular way, giving you all kinds of contextual cues about what you might skip, and about what everyone who reads this text needs. We could also use knowledge about how users find parts of sites though search, so that we could attract the people who are interested in the information in some of the modules. And we could look and see how users are clicking on a site to determine what is more popular and what tends to be skipped. On the Web, we can know all these things about how content becomes relevant to our users. In print, one thing we can do is to supply graphics and sidebars to help you skip the parts of this work that you don't need. But the static medium is a poor substitute for properly presented Web information.

When you write content explicitly for search engines (so that your users will find that content), in a sense, you invoke them with a compelling mix of keywords and links that draws users to your pages. The challenge is to craft your pages in ways that attract specific users from search engines, especially Google. In so doing, you can present relevant information to your audience. This book is about attracting your audience with keywords and links and thereby providing relevant information to them. As mentioned earlier, because search engine results cater to the way users scan and retrieve content on the Web, writing for search engines is also an effective way to write relevant content for your audience.

What Is Relevance on the Web?

The study of relevance is messy and complicated. But there's no running from it. If you want to be successful in writing for Web scanners and readers, you have to come to an understanding of how these people determine relevance on the Web. Like other aspects of the distinction between the oral, print, and Web contexts, how relevance is determined depends on the medium. But there are some common elements to the way relevance is determined in general. Though this book is about relevance on the Web, it's instructive to consider the more familiar oral and print contexts. We can then use comparison and contrast to show the different ways relevance works, depending on the medium.

The relevance of a statement, sentence, or fragment is determined by *the context of the communication that surrounds it*. In oral contexts, this means that what was said prior to a statement in part determines the relevance of that statement. In print contexts, the relevance of a sentence is determined by the sentences and paragraphs surrounding it. And in Web contexts, the relevance of a piece of content is determined by the elements of the page on which it appears, and by how that page relates to other pages, both internal and external. For a user, the context of a Web page is the last few pages he or she visited before visiting it. The page that referred a user to your page will give the user the strongest sense of your page's relevance. Something two clicks before your page will give a lesser sense, and so on. But because the user could come to your page from just about any other page on the Web, only some of which you have knowledge or control over, relevance is a particular challenge in Web publishing.

So what happens when a user comes to your carefully planned site from another site, such as a search engine? All the assumptions you have made about what is relevant to your users will not hold true. That user will not have followed your hierarchy of topics from the highest level to the lowest level. The user will land on your page cold. Unless your page can stand on its own for this kind of user, he or she will not find it relevant and will bounce off it. This often happens because many pages cannot stand on their own—they depend so crucially on other pages in their Web site's hierarchy that they make little sense to users who come to them from search engines or other external links.

Like it or not, most users use search to find what they're looking for on the Web. It is simply the quickest and easiest way to zero in on the most relevant information. Try as you may to control their activities and give them necessary background information through clear site architecture, they will ignore it and go straight to the answers to their questions or the solutions to their problems. Even those who come to a page on your site from its home page will often use your site's search function if the site is at all complicated. If your site search doesn't give them relevant results, they will often revert to Google. When Web content producers fail to produce relevant content for their users, it's generally because they didn't realize the vital importance of search on the Web.

As we indicated in Chapter 2, the crucial role of search is the root of the differences between print and Web media. Each page on a site must be able to show search users that it is relevant to them. This leads to a simple yet powerful tactic, which can turn ineffective Web sites into effective ones: Develop your content to be relevant for users who land on your pages from search engines, and it will be relevant to the majority of your users. The converse is also true: If you do not take search users into account when you develop your pages, the majority of your users will not find your content relevant.

Defining Relevance in Terms of Search

A good question to ask here is: What is relevance? For a piece of content on the Web, relevance can be defined as it applies to search engines. In this book, we focus on Google because it is the most used search engine on the planet. Bing is a good search engine that is gaining some traction in the search market. Baidu is the leader in China. Other countries have local search engines. But Google is the clear market leader, so it has earned our focus.

Perhaps Google's own definition of relevance can help. Google has put its quasi-definition of relevance on its site:

> That which has a logical or rational relation with something else, such as with the matter under discussion or a claim being investigated, etc., or has some bearing on or importance concerning real-world issues or current events.[1]

This is not very helpful. It says what we have already indicated: Relevance is a relational concept between a linguistic item and its context. For example, two sentences are

---

1. Taken from www.google.com/notebook/public/07491261619920101511/BDRreIgoQ853VyIsi. We call this a "quasi-definition" because it has numerous problems of definitional form. First, this definition is circular. Second, it does not encapsulate the meaning of the word relevance, but only gives examples of relevant things. Third, some of the examples treat relevance not as a relational concept but as an absolute ("concerning real-world issues or current events"), which violates its own definitional criterion.

relevant to each other if they're logically related, just as scientific evidence is logically related to a conclusion. But this is still not helpful. Relevance for writers is not about the semantic qualities of two pieces of text. It is about crafting content that will meet their audience's needs. By removing the individuals from its description, Google removes the central aspect of relevance for writers—the reader/writer relationship. In short, though the relational concept discussed in this definition gives us hints, it doesn't give us much understanding.

A better approach is to describe cases involving search and see what makes a page relevant to a user. To do this, we need to give an example of a success and an example of failure. We define *success* as having a user land on a page that he or she deems relevant and then become engaged with that page—by clicking something. We define *failure* in terms of bounce: If a user bounces off a page within a few seconds, he or she finds the content irrelevant, and the page has failed.

Given the above definitions, here are examples of success and failure.

Success: Suppose a user enters a phrase—say SOA—into Google's search field and clicks **Search.** When the user gets the search results, she clicks one on the first page and lands on a page that she deems relevant to the search query—say, IBM's main page on Service Oriented Architecture. The user then indicates relevance by clicking one of the calls to action on the page.

Failure: A user likewise engages Google's search application by entering SOA into the search field and gets pages of results. Clicking a result on the first page lands the user on the same IBM page, but this time the user finds the page completely irrelevant. He was looking for pages related to the Society of Actuaries, not Service Oriented Architecture. Having failed to read the short description of *SOA* from IBM on the search results page, he clicked the result anyway, landing on the irrelevant page. The user then indicates that the page is irrelevant by immediately clicking the **Back** button.

Before refining our definition, we don't want to lose a key insight from this example. Because there are so many different meanings for the same strings of letters (e.g., *SOA*), Google often can't divine what a user means by a particular search string and must make what amounts to a best guess. It does this by seeing what use its users tend to make of the words they enter into search strings. Google tracks whether users bounce off a page or engage with it. If its users bounce from pages that define *SOA* as *Society of Actuaries* more often than as *Service Oriented Architecture*, Google will guess that the majority of users mean *Service Oriented Architecture* when they type *SOA*. This is not only true of acronyms and other abbreviations, but of whole-word synonyms. Google makes similar probabilistic decisions based on a host of linguistic complexities in natural language. For this reason, its algorithm is not just the semantic concept that we quote above. It also includes all kinds of contextual effects, such as links, which determine how its users use the Web to communicate. We will return to these complexities later in the book.

Note that requiring engagement narrows our definition of relevance. A user might land on a relevant page and bounce off because she had already consumed all the information on it. So, although the page was relevant to her, it was no longer relevant enough to be worth her time. So she then clicks the **Back** button. This example demonstrates an important part of relevance that no purely semantic concept can capture: Relevance is not an absolute concept. Items are more or less relevant to users. Whether they choose to indicate with their clicks that a page is relevant to them is a matter of whether it is relevant *enough*. Web users are typically impatient, and their patience is variable. A page must be strongly relevant to a user to entice her to click one of its calls to action. That's why we narrow the definition of relevance considerably when we require engagement in our functional definition.

We will put the gory details of the linguistic underpinnings of relevance in a sidebar. Those skeptics among our readers who are inclined to dismiss our views because we use a functional definition can consult the sidebar (and the texts it refers to, if necessary). Those willing to give us the benefit of the doubt only need to know that the study of relevance is part of the field of **pragmatics**, the part of linguistics that deals with contextual effects, with how the semantic value of elements such as sentences and statements change from one context to another. Dan Sperber and Deirdre Wilson wrote the definitive text on the subject of relevance—aptly called *Relevance* (1986). It forms the basis for the following definition of relevance (adjusting their terminology to suit our needs).

1. A piece of content is relevant in a context to the extent that its contextual effects in the context are large.
2. A piece of content is relevant in a context to the extent that the effort required to process it in the context is small (Sperber and Wilson 1986, 125).

The only thing left is to explain in layman's terms what Sperber and Wilson mean here. First, consider that this definition contains **extent conditions,** which state the realm in which something is relevant. In other words, relevance is not an absolute either/or consideration, but a matter of degree. Second, the first extent condition is positive; it defines to what extent a piece of content is relevant. A piece of content is relevant to the extent that it causes a large change in the audience. The second condition is negative; it defines how relevance is limited by matters such as time, space, attention, and patience. A piece of content is relevant to the extent that it requires little effort (time or attention, for example) to grasp it and act on it.

But what is a contextual effect? It is a change in the audience. Sperber and Wilson define contextual effects in cognitive terms, that is, in terms of the audience's mental state. If the audience has an epiphany, that is a large contextual effect. If the audience merely tweaks one of its beliefs, that is a small contextual effect. However, for our purposes, we will not talk about the audience's cognitive states. Instead, we will only talk about audience *behavior*, because that is the only thing we can measure. It is likely that every click from a user results in some change in her brain state (and some users click mindlessly). But we are nowhere near smart enough to know what that change is or how to measure it, especially in such complex creatures as humans. So, for our purposes, concentrating on functional/behavioral contextual effects will do.

The Linguistics of Relevance

Sperber and Wilson (1986) focus on Paul Grice's line of thought (1957), which holds that communication is often a matter of inferring the intentions of a speaker based on the context of an utterance. The context might include any number of features, including the physical space of the speaker and hearer, what was previously said between them, their histories, and what they know about each other. The basis of their book *Relevance* is essentially that relevance is a matter of such inferences. In other words, utterances are relevant to a hearer to the extent that the hearer infers their meaning from the many facts surrounding the communication.

Before we explain their approach, here are a few notes on terminology.

- An **assumption** is a technical term for assertions, facts, etc. These are things that the audience believes.

- By **consequences**, Sperber and Wilson mean the inferential process of relating assumptions.

- A **contextual effect** is the change in existing assumptions based on a new assumption. These effects can be in the form of contextual implications, contradictions, and strengthenings.

- Sperber and Wilson argue that "having contextual effects is a necessary condition for relevance, and that other things being equal, the greater the contextual effect, the greater the relevance" (Sperber and Wilson 1986, 119).

For example, suppose you live at a time when the prevailing view is that the earth is flat. So your dominant assumption relative to the shape of the earth is that it looks like a coin. But you attend a lecture by Copernicus in which he demonstrates fairly conclusively that the earth is round. This has a strong contradictory contextual effect on your dominant assumption. It is therefore highly relevant. And suppose it is enough to convince you provisionally. Then, news from explorers such as Columbus and Magellan proves beyond much doubt that the earth is indeed round, which has a strong strengthening contextual effect on your provisional view that the earth is round. Finally, Galileo demonstrates that the earth is not exactly round, but is somewhat thicker in the middle (through his observations of lunar eclipses). This has a strong contextual implication, which modifies your belief that the earth is round. All

continues

three types of contextual effect are strong, and therefore the assumptions related to them are highly relevant to your understanding of the geometry of the earth.

The key phrase in the last bullet above is "other things being equal." The second aspect that mitigates relevance is *effort*. Effort is friction for relevance. In other words, the more effort it takes to process a contextual effect, the less relevant it is to the audience. In the above example, it required a great deal of effort to move from the notion that the earth is flat to the notion that the earth is round. So even though Copernicus had the largest contextual effect, he also required the greatest amount of processing effort. This effort would be even greater if you were just passing by the place where he was talking and had little interest in the topic, as opposed to being a student of earth sciences. Galileo's discovery, which simply changed the idea of "roundness" somewhat, might not have had as large a contextual effect as that of Copernicus, but it also required the least amount of effort. Relative to each other, Copernicus and Galileo might be deemed equally relevant here, depending on other characteristics of the audience, such as interest level, encyclopedic knowledge, and so on.

With that, here are the two extent conditions for relevance.

1. An assumption is relevant in a context to the extent that its contextual effects in the context are large.

2. An assumption is relevant in a context to the extent that the effort required to process it in the context is small (Sperber and Wilson 1986, 125).

Notice that these are not criteria for relevance, in the sense that they don't *define* what is relevant or not. Rather, these are extent conditions: They define to what extent something is or is not relevant. In that sense, Sperber and Wilson are not trying to develop a cognitive or psychological theory that is universally applicable to all communicators. They are merely developing useful tools to help us understand how relevance works in such nonrepresentational ways.

> Relevance is a property which need not be represented, let alone computed, in order to be achieved. When it is represented, it is represented in terms of comparative judgments and gross absolute judgments, (e.g., 'irrelevant', 'weakly relevant', 'very relevant'), but not in terms of fine absolute judgments, i.e., quantitative ones (Sperber and Wilson 1986, 132).

Another way of saying this is that relevance is not absolute; it is relative to a number of variables. These variables can be described in terms of the audiences' discourse communities, past educations, language and culture of origin, interest levels, learning disabilities, and so forth. The common outward characteristics of audiences define to what extent a given set of words is relevant to them.

Sperber and Wilson's treatment of relevance is not controversial for oral communication. But the question is, to what extent does it work in print or Web contexts?

They contended that it worked in all media—a claim that requires much more study. We are skeptical that it applies uniformly across media, considering that other fields of language study are influenced by the variable of the medium. Grammar, for example, changed greatly when the uniform practice of spaces between words was implemented across the western world.

However, applying Sperber and Wilson rigorously to Web contexts is the subject of another course of study. Therefore, assume that we are using the Sperber and Wilson model provisionally here. It seems to work; all we really need is a functional definition for the purposes of this book. But it has not been rigorously tested in an academic setting. Enterprising readers in academic settings are hereby encouraged to take up this challenge.

So far we have defined relevance in terms of user interactions with Google. You might think this odd. We could easily define it in terms of how different pages relate to each other in a site's architecture. There are any number of other ways we could have tried to define it as well. Why use search as the central concept? One reason we have already given is that many users start looking for information at Google and other search engines. So this seems a likely place to start. But there is another key reason that Sperber and Wilson's work suggests: All things considered, the less effort it takes to find the information you need, the more relevant it is. These two reasons are related: Google is popular because it tends to produce relevant results in Sperber and Wilson's sense. That is, more than any other Web application, it tends to help users find content with the least effort and the largest contextual effect.

So our choice of search in general, and Google in specific, is not arbitrary. Google is the bellwether of relevance: If you want to create the most relevant content for Web audiences, write for Google first, and take care of all other aspects of effective Web content later. That is the central thesis of this book. But what does it mean? How do you write for Google first? Read on to find out.

On Writing Relevant Content for Web Users

We will go into the specifics of our Google-first methodology in later chapters. But let us sketch the approach here.

In most publishing environments, we decide what and how we want to communicate with our target audience. We design messages that we think will engage that audience and inspire them to act in ways we desire. We then define successful communication by what percentage of our target audience acts the way we hope it will (such as purchasing ads, writing a paper that complements ours, purchasing a product, or writing a review). The Google-first methodology does not reject this basic process; it turns it on its head.

A common mistake in writing for the Web is to optimize content after the fact. Again, based on the model of crafting a message that you want to communicate and following the other steps in the chain, the last step is to prepare the content for the Web. Many content producers only consider search optimization after they have determined *what* they want to communicate. They take existing pages, do some keyword research, and map the pages to the relevant keywords that are most often typed in Google's search field. Then they add those words at the appropriate places on the page.

The problem with this approach is it does not take into account that the content on the page doesn't necessarily match the keywords very well. In some cases, the words you choose as you write happen to be the ones that searchers use. But that is rare. In many cases, especially in large corporate organizations with their own cultures and terminologies, the words that writers choose to communicate their messages *do not* match those that searchers use. If you optimize a page after the fact, the words you put in the title tag, the heading, and so on might not match the body copy of the page you wrote. Users may be attracted to one of your pages, but many of those who come to it from search will bounce off it when they determine that the content of the page is not relevant to their chosen keyword.

In extreme cases, Google will look at this after-the-fact process and see manipulation. Google has a filter for such efforts, and it will expunge your page from its index if you try too hard to optimize for content after the fact. One of the reasons Google is the search leader is that it aggressively filters out those who maniplate its algorithm by trying too hard to optimize pages after they are written (intentionally or not). This makes sense, because Google's audience consists of search users. Google measures success based on the relevance of the results to the search terms that users type into its search field. If its users find the results of their search efforts irrelevant, they might try another search engine. Expunging irrelevant results from its index is a key tactic for Google to stay ahead of the competition. The other primary way that it competes is by determining that the chosen keywords for a page are tightly relevant to what the page is about. If you optimize after the fact, Google might still index your page and even display it to users, but it will not rank among the top pages for that keyword. Indeed, it probably won't be anywhere in the top five pages of search results. For all intents and purposes, then, your content will be irrelevant to your target audience.

Unlike with other media, we do not have control over who consumes our messages on the Web. Targeting their audience precisely, PR folks send press releases to media representatives, marketing folks send direct mailers to an approved list of customers and prospective customers, sales people send proposals to known leads, and academics write for a known audience of journal subscribers. But on the Web, anybody or nobody might find your content in the first place. And those who do find it might consider it irrelevant on first glance. So attracting the target audience comes first. And, as we have demonstrated, the best way to attract the target audience is by optimizing your content for Google. This means performing keyword research before you even start writing, and determining what to write, how to write it, and how to deliver it to Web users based on your keyword research.

If you do this properly, you will not simply attract whoever comes to your site from Google and hope for the best, as many search engine optimists recommend. Instead, by proceeding correctly, you will attract an audience that is likely to engage in your content and perform the actions you desire them to. Part of the transformation from the print model to the Web model is adjusting expectations. Direct mail is considered a success if 1 percent of the audience takes the desired action. Magazine advertisers are often happy to get 50 new leads out of 50,000 readers. But on the Web, you can expect the majority of your users to engage with your site if you do your keyword research and craft a structure of pages to serve their content needs.

As you begin to consider turning the publishing process on its head in writing for the Web, consider the main benefit of starting with keyword research and developing pages only after you learn how the target audience uses language: Keyword research is a powerful way to analyze your audience. In print contexts, you might form a fictional picture of your target audience based on their backgrounds and assumed shared knowledge. But still, you are choosing to communicate with them using just your words. But you can never be sure that your word choices will match audiences' word usage.

On the Web, you learn how your target audience uses language and you address them with their own words. Done right, keyword research can let you precisely bridge the gap between your messages and your audiences' needs.

Summary

- The Web opens a new avenue for audience analysis. Unlike print, where we must form fictional pictures of our audience and guess how best to invoke this audience, by doing keyword research before creating our content, we can address our target audience with their very own words.

- For all intents and purposes, relevance on the Web can be defined by the behavior of users coming from Google. To the extent that users come to your site from Google and engage with your content by clicking its links, you can determine how relevant your content is to your target audience.

- These two principles lead to the central thesis of this book: The most effective way to create Web content is to take a search-first approach.

  1. Define your target audience and perform keyword research to see what terms they use to find relevant content on the Web.

  2. Develop a list of core words that your target audience uses and write one page for each of those words.

  3. Test your pages to ensure relevance, and adjust as necessary.

- If you adopt a search-first approach for the Web, you can realistically increase your expectations about audience engagement. Whereas you might be satisfied with 1 percent engagement with some print efforts, you can shoot for 50 percent engagement rates or better on the Web. Unlike print, you can tune your pages to improve engagement rates as time goes on.

CHAPTER **4**

Discovering and Using Keywords to Attract Your Target Audience

As we indicated in Chapter 3, the search-first writing methodology begins with keyword research, after which you write pages to attract your target audience and address their needs with relevant content. The two inputs to your writing plan are a description of the target audience and a set of keywords that the target audience is likely to use. Armed with this information, writing Web content that is optimized for search engines—particularly Google—is a fairly simple matter of making sure Google's crawler can find the keywords in strategic places on your pages. This chapter covers those three tactics, along with some necessary background information on the linguistics of search engines:

- Defining your target audience
- Linguistic considerations for keywords
- Discovering the keywords related to your topic that the audience most often uses
- Developing Web content with those keywords in strategic places on your pages

Defining the Target Audience

Defining your target audience is another aspect of Web writing that does not resemble many print contexts. In public relations, the writer develops a list of press analysts, editors, and publishers and writes press releases for them. In sales, the writer typically has a lot of information about the client for whom the sales proposal is written. Grant writers have details about the reviewers for their grant proposals before they write.

Those are just a few of the cases in the print medium in which the audience is well known. There are also many more cases in which you really know very little about your audience in print, except perhaps that they are interested in what you write. If they are not interested in what you write, they will stop reading. But this is not very helpful in crafting messages that appeal to their needs. When we form a picture of our audience, we strive to understand things such as their prior knowledge, common experiences, shared beliefs, and shared assumptions, so that we can use these traits to engage the reader, and to narrow our focus to what the reader needs. In short, given what we know about our audience, we want to maximize relevance for them. A corollary of this is that we also want to minimize what is irrelevant to the reader. Irrelevant content acts as friction and distracts readers from getting what they need.

Whether you know a lot or a little about your target audience in print, your audience analysis vastly differs from Web audience analysis. In print, you discover who reads the publication for which you are writing and try to appeal to their common traits. Lacking such knowledge, you engage them with compelling storytelling techniques, compelling them to do things your way. But on the Web, you don't simply discover traits about your target audience. You define your target audience by some common traits and seek to attract only people who have those traits to your site. Print is passive; the Web is active. When you are confident that you are attracting your target audience to your pages, you are free to address them and use their defined traits as the common ground that you need to achieve mutual understanding.

Web audience analysis is less about *discovering* common audience traits than about *defining* them. In passive media such as print, you discover common audience traits (such as subscribing to a vertical journal) and use these traits to help you make assumptions about their common knowledge. These assumptions help you focus on what they need, rather than writing for the least common denominator. But in active media such as the Web, you can't make these assumptions as readily because of the diversity of the audience. So you are forced to define the audience that you want to attract and write in ways that will tend to attract that audience through search.

When you define audience traits, you simply identify the interests of your target audience. For example, suppose you have a writing and editing service and want to attract clients who are interested in this kind of offering. If you narrow your focus on this simple trait, your audience might be highly diverse, but they have one trait in common—they need writing and editing services. Unlike with print, the more you narrow your definition of your target, the more effective your Web writing will be. If you try to associate the main trait you seek with a set of likely complementary traits, you risk writing irrelevant content for those who do not share those complementary traits.

Common Web Audience Characteristics

In this chapter, we make the simplifying assumption that all you know about your audience is that they came to your page using keywords in a search engine. Given this, in Chapter 5 we will delve into ways to deepen your audience knowledge. But for the present we'll only discuss keyword knowledge, to see just how much knowledge you actually have if all you know about your audience is that they came to your site from a search engine by using keywords. When we look into this assumption, you will find that keyword knowledge is a lot richer than you might think at first. Still, it is necessary to deal with the fact that Web audiences are much more diverse than print audiences, and to provide some baseline descriptions that will help you craft messages for the many diverse individuals who come to your content from search engines.

Here are some Web audience characteristics that Web writers at IBM find helpful to have in mind as they write. Web readers are

- **Diverse:** It's called the World Wide Web because people from all over the world access your content and need to understand it. This does not mean that you must do a lot of translation and search optimization in other languages. But it does mean that you must write in ways that non-native speakers of English can understand. If you use a lot of local idioms or other culture-centric language, you will lose your audience and be subject to the dreaded bounce.

- **Engaged:** The Web is not just an information publishing medium. It's an interactive application through which information is communicated and transactions are made. Many Web users don't care for static experiences. If you have static content that will be relevant for a month or more, publish it in PDF format and put a description and a link to it on your Web page. Reserve your Web content for things that will inspire your visitors to *do* something, even if it's just to download and print a PDF file.

- **Intelligent:** When addressing a diverse audience, writers often tend to write to the least common denominator, or to "dumb it down." This is a mistake. You can write clear content for diverse audiences without patronizing them with sentences for third graders. Don't avoid complex and challenging topics; just explain them in clear, straightforward ways.

- **Skeptical:** Unless you write for well-known sites such as Wikipedia, chances are that your site has not yet gained the credibility of your diverse audience. (At one time Wikipedia didn't have a lot of credibility either.) This is especially true of users who come to your content from search (as opposed to bookmarks or external trusted links). You don't just *write* content for the Web, you *prove* it. If you can't at least demonstrate that your content is plausible (through links to trusted sources or your own proof points), don't bother writing it.

- **Time challenged:** We've said this in many other ways in this book, but it bears repeating. Web readers expect information design and writing to be efficient. In print contexts, you might need a lot of fluffy language to draw readers into the story and entice them to keep reading. On the Web, though, this has precisely the opposite effect, especially at the higher levels. Don't use this kind of language until

continues

users have demonstrated with their clicks that they are willing to engage in print-centric reading. Even then, use it with caution. Remember, users can come to your lowest-level content through search.

- **Unique:** Although your audience is diverse on the Web, it is also typically casual and informal. Social media has changed the expectations of Web users, whether they come to your site from social media contexts or from more traditional Web publishing environments, such as search engines. They now expect you to engage them in a conversational tone, and as unique individuals. They also expect to be given a space to comment or otherwise enter feedback, and to engage in conversation with other users of the site.

For the moment, let's assume that the only thing you know about your audience is that they came to your site from Google using keywords that you coded into your pages. That doesn't seem like a lot of information to go on. However, as you follow our information path through this book, you will find that it is more than you might think. It is just a simplifying assumption. We will go into depth about what you can know about your audience, and how to gain this knowledge in Chapter 5. But if you only know that your users came to your site from Google using certain keyword phrases, you know that most content topics related to those keywords will likely be relevant. We'll explore this here by explaining how to design information that will be maximally relevant for users who come to your pages from Google.

Some Linguistic Considerations Related to Keywords

Until now, we have talked about the keywords that your target audience enters into search fields, without talking about *what keywords are* and *how they work* so that Google can identify relevant content. Strictly speaking, keywords are strings of characters that people enter into search fields. Actually, it is a bit of a misnomer to call them "keywords," because many users enter phrases or word combinations into search fields, to try to zero in on the most relevant content. The shorter the string of characters entered, the less likely it is that the search will return relevant results. On the other hand, as we have mentioned before, sophisticated search users enter *long-tail keywords* because the longer and more complex the search string, the more likely the result will be relevant.

Google indexes Web content by keywords. When a user enters a keyword string into a search field, Google uses its algorithm to determine the most relevant content in its index for the search term. We will delve into further aspects of the Google algorithm later in this chapter, but for now, think of it as a matching algorithm. If a user enters a string that exactly matches the keywords that Google associates with a piece of content in its index, there's a good chance that piece of content will appear in the first few pages of results. If there are no exact matches, Google tries to match parts and pieces of a keyword string to the content in its index. This means that unless a query is made using the advanced search function, Google's algorithm will associate any of the words in a keyword string to find the best matches, in any combination.

Users of Google's advanced search function can use Boolean specifications to designate not only the *words* in a keyword phrase, but also *the logic of their combination* (Figure 4.1). For example, Google's **Advanced Search** screen has a field with "*all these words*" as its label. If a user enters `ibm developer soa` in that field, Google will only find pages that contain all those words. Users can also exclude content by putting words to *exclude* in the appropriate field. Another trick for queries is to use quotation marks to tell Google to only show content with that exact phrase; Entering `"ibm soa"` (including the quote marks) will only return phrases that contain that particular phrase.

If users don't get the desired results from a keyword string, they often go back and modify the string. For example, a novice user might enter the word `blue` in a search field. For such a vague search term, Google might return a staggeringly huge number of results, none of which would be useful. So, the user might go back and enter `Big Blue`, indicating that she's not just interested in the color, but in one of its many associations, this time with IBM. And she could further refine her keyword string to narrow her search through trial and error. Users often find content this way: They start with vague, generic terms and gradually narrow their search down by adding modifiers.

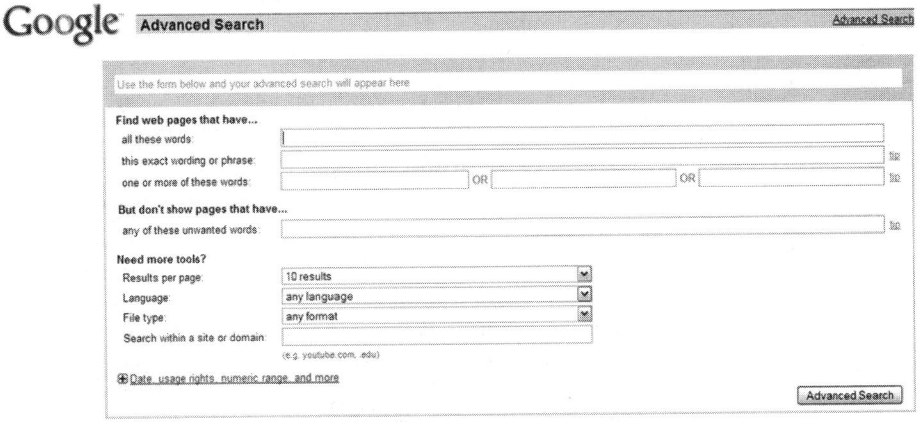

Figure 4.1   The Google Advanced Search Application. (*Source:* /www.google.com/advanced_search?hl=en)

We assume that you have some experience using search engines. In particular, you might have had the experience of trying to find content related to a keyword and finding the results completely different than you anticipated. Typically, this happens when Google has a hard time interpreting your search query. Why? Well, natural language is extremely complex—too complex for computers to divine the meaning of a few words taken out of context (see Figure 4.2). In particular, a lot of words have multiple literal meanings, called **homonyms**. Read the dictionary to see several definitions for the same word, and you can begin to understand the challenge. Another common set of linguistic complexity is called **homographs**: words that share the same spelling but are pronounced differently. For example, the words *lead* (as in *leadership*) and *lead* (as in *pencil lead*) look identical to Google unless they are put in the context of their parts of speech, prefixes or suffixes. Many more variations on homographs can be found in the English language. (See the sidebar for a more complete discussion of the variations.) We won't delve too deeply into the complexity here. Suffice it to say that the most effective keywords have some of this context built in (with prefixes, suffixes, and use of various parts of speech).

Limiting Ambiguity: Linguistic Concerns in Keyword Research

One intent of keyword research is to limit ambiguity. Linguistic complexity can foster ambiguity, which needs to be addressed with your target audience in mind. In other words, you have to be sensitive to the use of homonyms and related linguistic concepts in your keyword research. Being sensitive to this aspect of terminology confusion will greatly benefit your keyword research and audience definition.

Homonyms

Homonyms are words that sound alike but have different meanings or spellings. There are three kinds:

- *Homonyms*, words that sound and look alike (*bank* as in a slope, *bank* as in a place for money, and *bank* as in a bench or row of switches)

- *Homophones*, words that sound alike but do not look alike (*meet, meat*)

- *Homographs*, words that look alike but do not sound alike (the verb *lead*, the metal *lead*)

Source: http://grammar.about.com/od/fh/g/homonymterm.htm

For homonyms, linguistic ambiguity is mostly an issue with broad or single-word keywords. An example of this can be seen in *Mustang* (the car) or *mustang* (the horse). One way to limit the ambiguity from this example is to include adjectives and nouns, further refining the keyword phrase with a greater level of specificity.

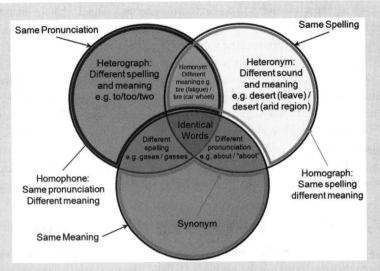

Figure 4.2   A graph of linguistic complexities related to keywords. (*Source:* http://en.wikipedia.org/wiki/Homonyms)

For more information on these topics, see http://ezinearticles.com/?Homograph, -Homonym,-or-Homophone?&id=275667 and http://en.wikipedia.org/wiki/Homonyms.

Permutations

Another type of complexity is in how keyword phrases are put together. The longer the phrase, the more permutations it can have. For example, the terms *business, networking,* and *group* can be entered in six different ways:

Business networking group

Business group networking

Networking business group

Networking group business

Group business networking

Group networking business

Note that the meaning of the phrase changes with different word order. For this reason, you need to try the different combinations of words in your keyword research to see which ones are more popular and competitive. And try them out in search engines to see if your target audience will find the combination relevant. If the content Google returns in a search is relevant to your target audience, it is a good choice, all things considered.

It's hard to take a few words in a search string and understand what the searcher meant by them. And once the computer makes an educated guess, it is even harder to find the most relevant content for that meaning. The same keyword with the same meaning is typically highly relevant only to a subset of the population, and totally irrelevant to the rest. Google is a marvel of human ingenuity because it does a pretty good job not only of divining the meaning of a search query, but of providing relevant search results. But not all of that is linguistic. About half of Google's algorithm deals with the popularity or link equity of pages in its index. This helps Google determine the pages most likely to be relevant to the searcher. We will discuss PageRank in Chapter 7. For now, it's enough to know that Google doesn't simply rely on the semantics (the linguistics of meaning) of search strings, but also builds a context around the pages in its index by considering such extra-linguistic features as links.

Discovering Keywords Used by Your Target Audience

The central aspect of search-first writing is to connect with your target audience by crafting Web experiences using what you know about Google. The first step in this process is called **keyword discovery** or **keyword research**. Many Web publishers assume that they should just write what they want to communicate and let the search engines naturally find their content. This works if the vocabulary you use happens to coincide with the vocabulary your target audience uses to find pages of interest in Google. However, in our experience, creating search-optimized content by accident rarely happens. Especially when writing in marketing settings, writers often fail to realize that their company's specific vocabulary pervades their writing. This means that the writers are using too much specialized, branded language. This neglects search optimization or leaves it to chance, which produces very poor results. Don't leave your search optimization to chance this way.

By using keyword research, you can gain some measure of control over search optimization by ensuring that the vocabulary you use on your pages is the same as that of your target audience. Keyword research tells you how many people searched on a particular term in a given month. This is not the only information you need, but it is a starting point. If you don't do keyword research, you can own the top position in Google for a term that very few people search on but get very little traffic to your pages as a result. If you use a coined or branded term, chances are that people who find your page from Google will find it relevant to them. That might be good enough for certain circumstances, but it is not good enough for most. Keyword research can help you discover the terms that are both relevant to your target audience and get a relatively high volume of traffic. That is the goal of keyword research.

On the other end of the scale, you can rank well for words that lots of users search on and get lots of traffic to your pages as a result. But if most of those users bounce off your pages, indicating that they find the content irrelevant, you will need to find terms that are more relevant to your target audience. It is better to have decent levels of traffic with low bounce rates than high levels of traffic with a lot of bounce. Each time that users bounce off your page, you leave a negative impression in their minds, and you hurt your ranking in Google. On the other hand, each user who comes to your page and is drawn to engage with your content by clicking your links will have a positive experience. Again, the goal is to combine relatively high traffic with relatively low bounce rates, because ultimately, low bounce rates tend to lead to high engagement rates. Engagement is the best way to measure the relevance of your content for your target audience. (We discuss how to measure bounce and engagement in Chapter 9).

You can't do your keyword research just once, though. If you find high bounce rates, you will need to revisit your content, choose new keywords and republish—and do more keyboard research. Page-level research and keyword research are iterative processes. From your initial keyword research, you can make a good educated guess as to which terms your target audience is most likely to use when searching for content. But this initial guess often misses the mark. Then, you need to do deeper keyword research and craft content that better targets your audience. So, keyword research should be a central part of your everyday Web operations. In particular, it should always precede the writing of each piece of your Web content. It is better to write with the keywords that your target audience uses than to retrofit content with keywords after the fact, keywords which may not perfectly match the content you've created. The good news is that if your initial research misses the mark, the power of the Web allows you to make changes and republish relatively easily. Take advantage of that power.

Case Study: IBM Smarter Planet Search Efforts

In 2009 IBM launched an initiative to lead the industry in helping to solve large problems facing the world, such as climate change. IBM branded this effort "Smarter Planet." It created content to help organizations understand how to use technology to better manage healthcare, traffic, energy, agriculture, infrastructure, and similar large-scale efforts. The content was created to raise awareness of important issues facing the planet, and to encourage a more general audience to try to solve some of these problems with technology.

From a search perspective, this is a challenging content model. In a lot of IBM marketing contexts, content is written to support an established brand, such as *DB2*. A Web content effort to support IBM's DB2 information management software might contain separate pages to drive demand for branded product, and to raise the awareness of users who search on targeted keywords when considering this type of software, such as the term *database software*. Search optimization with branded terms is relatively easy. For example, users who search on *DB2* are likely to engage with a page that contains it. But if users search on the generic term *database software* as a

continues

general term, they are less likely to engage with pages that have DB2 content than those who searched on the branded keyword. That's because they might be more interested in other database software offerings. However, in the time span covered in Figure 4.3, hundreds of thousands of users searched on *database software* every month, while only about 18,000 searched for "DB2." But notice the high click rate for DB2. If you have a branded term with the brand equity of DB2, you know you'll get high demand-generation engagement rates on that term. If you can also manage to build awareness with a certain percentage of users who searched on the generic term *database software*, you can count your search efforts as successful.

Keyword	Est. Searches per Month	Share of Clicks	Current Rank at Google
DB2 Information on Demand			
db2	18,618	38.48%	1
database software	214,760	0.00%	Not in top 30
database management	113,939	0.00%	Not in top 30
document management	1,618,298	0.00%	Not in top 30

Figure 4.3   IBM's search performance for four keywords. (*Source:* IBM Corp.)

In the case of Smarter Planet, there is no one brand to rely on—all your efforts are to build awareness of terms that have limited brand equity in the marketplace. The challenge with this content from a search perspective is easily understood by looking at the keywords that the team chose. Their first inclination was to use the terms that the writers used to describe the issues. For example, for a page with the heading *Smart Utilities*, the keyword chosen for the `<title>` tag was `<title>` *IBM– a smarter planet – utilities*`</title>`. *Users who searched on that exact string* in Google naturally *found* the content. *The problem was, however, that very few users searched on that exact string.*

After performing keyword research, the team determined that the best balance of branding and keyword value was the term *Smart Grid.* The research indicated that nearly 2,000 users searched on that term in a month. In addition, those who searched on the term were likely to be interested in the Smarter Planet content related to smart utilities. Fortunately, the only things that needed to be changed on the page were the `<title>` tag and the `<H1>` tag. The body copy already contained the words *smart* and *grid* in it. This is a bit unusual. Typically, if you make a keyword change, you also have to rewrite the copy to incorporate the new keyword into it. That is why it is always better to do your keyword research before you write the copy. You want to make sure your vocabulary is consistent with the vocabulary that your target audience uses to communicate about topics of interest, and to find content with Google.

Fortunately, the team performed keyword research prior to writing subsequent Smarter Planet content. This ensured that as soon as the content was published, it started receiving relatively high volumes of targeted traffic. In other words, the copy was optimally relevant for the audience, according to our search-first definition.

So you need to do your keyword research before writing. How do you do this? Conducting keyword research is a matter of figuring out what terms related to your topic are most often searched on and choosing the words or phrases from that list that you think your audience is most likely to use. As we indicated above, it is an iterative process—you make an educated guess and test your success, prepared to make adjustments to tune the relevance of your pages for your target audience.

Figuring out which terms are most often searched on is a matter of using tools such as Google AdWords to test possible words and phrases. There are dozens of tools (see the sidebar for a more complete list) for finding the most often-searched-on terms, with a variety of cost structures and feature sets, including the Keyword Discovery Tool (www .keyworddiscovery.com/start.html) or Aaron Wall's Free Keyword List Generator (http://tools.seobook.com/keyword-list/) to discover the demand for a keyword. Demand is a function of the number of users who search on a term in a given time frame, typically a month.

In addition to demand, you also need to measure competition for your keywords. Competition can be measured in several ways. But technically, it's the search strength of the pages that rank on Google's top page for your chosen keywords. The best way to learn this is simply by searching on the words and looking into the pages that rank well in Google. How well optimized are these pages? How interwoven are they in the topic or field surrounding them? A keyword that has lots of high-powered competition might not be your best choice. But some words are central to your mission, so you absolutely have to own them. *Smarter Planet* is such a keyword for IBM. So you do what it takes to rank well for those words.

A quick-and-dirty way to test the words that you think might be popular is simply by typing them into Google. As shown in Figure 4.4, under Google's default setting of "Provide query suggestions in the search box," you'll see various incremental possible matches for your search string, with the total number of "hits," while you type in your entries. This only gives you a rough estimate of the competition for the keywords. To get the information you need to determine competition, you'll have to use the tools that measure competition, such as Covario. Because we try to focus on free tools in this book, we will not delve into a description of Covario. Feel free to check it out on your own (www.covario.com/). Wordtracker (www.wordtracker.com/) has a free tool to help you measure keyword competition.

Figure 4.4   A quick-and-dirty keyword discovery tool to get a rough estimate of keyword competition from the Google search page. We recommend using Wordtracker or a similar tool to validate your initial keyword competition data. (*Source:* www.google.com)

Keyword Discovery Tools

No one can keep track of all the keyword tools on the market today. And no single tool gives you a complete picture of keyword demand and competition. However, we recommend using four main tools to come at the problem from four perspectives: Google AdWords, Google Insights, The Keyword Discovery Tool, and Aaron Wall's Advanced Keyword Research tool. We also include descriptions of other tools here in case you want to go deeper still into keyword research. These include the Keyword Density and Prominence Analyzer, Wordtracker, and Wikipedia's article traffic statistics tool. All of these tools are discussed below.

In addition to the tools listed below, consider researching your competitors for the keywords they use. An easy way to obtain a keyword list of competitors is to type keywords into Google to see what sites are ranking high. You can then research and analyze your "seed" words by using various free or paid keyword research tools. Below is a list of various free and paid tools. It is by no means comprehensive, but it could help you get started with your keyword discovery.

These tools are evolving and changing faster than a print book can keep up with them. So please note that the keyword tools landscape will likely have changed between the writing and printing of this book. One common trend is that free tools become paid tools as they gain popularity. So please also be advised that some of the tools we list as free might be paid as you read this.

1. **Google AdWords Keyword Tool:** https://adwords.google.com/select/Keyword-ToolExternal. This can help you get new keyword ideas. This tool is helpful for Web site content, as well as for Ad campaign keywords. It's a free tool that shows estimated traffic numbers and works best when used with short keywords, one or two words in length. You can also type in the URL of your competitor and Google AdWords will show the keywords your competitor is using (see Figure 4.5).

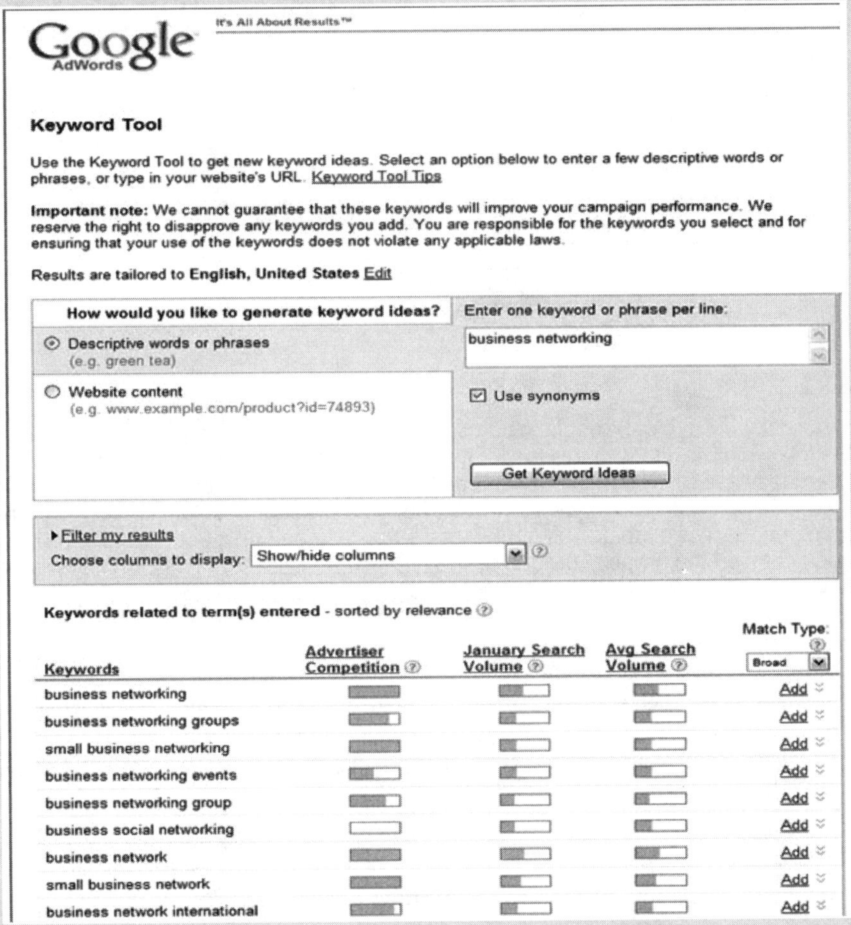

Figure 4.5   A Google AdWords Keyword tool output. Though the tool is designed for understanding the impact of a word on a Google ad campaign, it works as an organic keyword research tool as well. (*Source:* Google)

2. **Google Insights:** www.googleinsights.com. This tool lets you find keywords and emerging keywords in top searches and rising searches, but not actual volume (see

continues

Figure 4.6). It is scaled and normalized at 100%, so it measures interest level. You can gauge pertinent interest in specific keywords. These insights can help you determine which keywords resonate best, based on searcher interest.

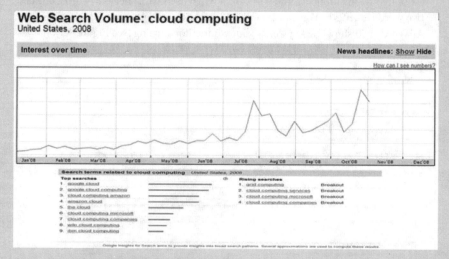

Figure 4.6   A typical Google Insights output. Note that Google Insights publishes the following proviso with this tool: "The numbers on the graph reflect how many searches have been done for a particular term, relative to the total number of searches done on Google over time. They don't represent absolute search volume numbers, because the data is normalized and presented on a scale from 0-100; each point on the graph is divided by the highest point, or 100. The numbers next to the search terms above the graph are summaries, or totals." (*Source:* Google)

3. **Keyword Discovery:** www.keyworddiscovery.com/login.html. This has free and paid versions, such as a Search Term Suggestion Tool that provides a good breadth and depth of terms (see Figure 4.7). It is a Web-based system that compiles search statistics from 180 search engines worldwide. Currently, the free version only allows you to import keyword results one word at a time, rather than from multiple keywords. Bulk import ability is also limited. For these reasons, we recommend paying for the better performance of the paid tool. The paid version also includes competitive analysis and competitive intelligence.

4. **Aaron Wall's Advanced Keyword Research Tool:** http://tools.seobook .com/keyword-tools/seobook/. This tool cross references Wordtracker, Google, Yahoo, and Bid Prices (see Figure 4.8). It shows estimated volumes in search engines by displaying and linking to related search results, semantically related phrases, and Quintura (described in Chapter 5).

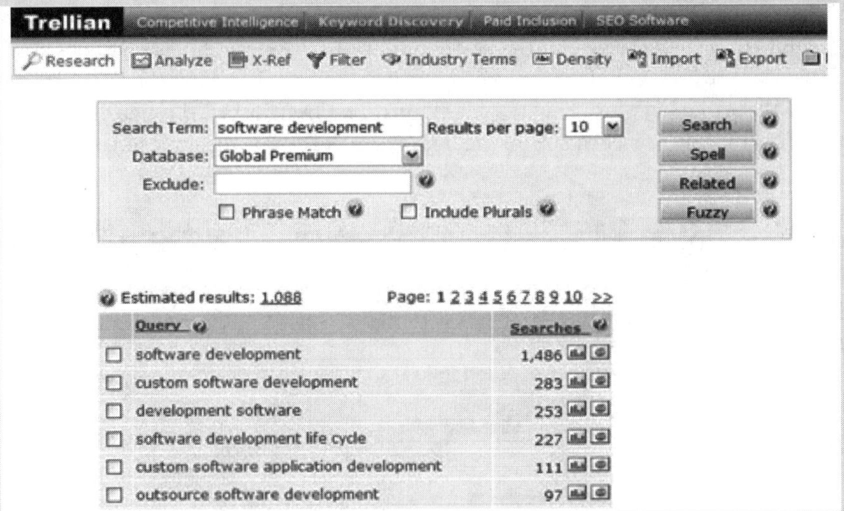

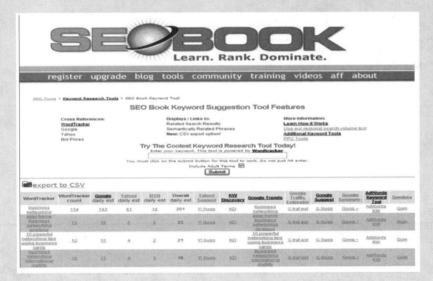

Figure 4.7   A typical output of the Trellian Keyword Discovery tool. (*Source:* www.trellian.com)

Figure 4.8   A typical output of Aaron Wall's Advanced Keyword Research tool. (*Source:* tools.seebook.com)

continues

5. **Keyword Density and Prominence Analyzer**, also known as **Ranks.nl.** Use
   this to do a competitive analysis and determine what keyword phrases your competitors are best optimized for (see Figure 4.9). You can just enter the URL and not
   use the actual keyword. Look for a Keyword Text Density of 2 through 10 and for
   Keyword Prominence of 80% or greater to help determine the topic of your page.

Figure 4.9   The Keyword Density and Prominence Analyzer input and output.
(*Source:* ranks.nl)

6. **Wordtracker:** http://freekeywords.wordtracker.com/. This tool helps you find the
   top keywords that you can use, based on Dogpile and Metacrawler. It eliminates
   bots as it looks at meta search engines, which is to say that it eliminates searches

from individuals who are not really part of your audience. It also can give you a sense of keyword competition, as well as demand (see Figure 4.10).

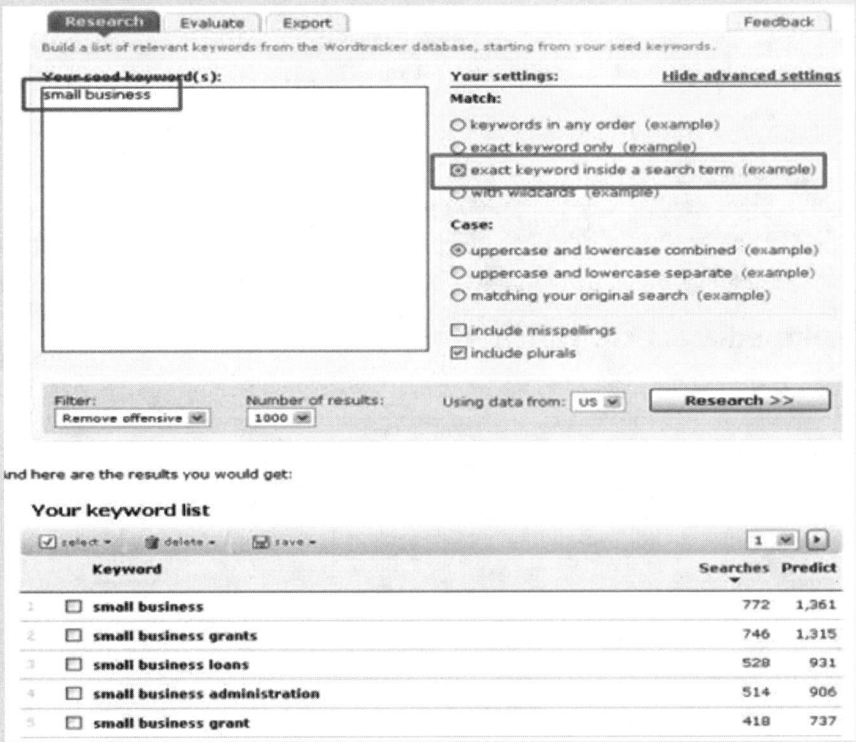

Figure 4.10   A Wordtracker output. (*Source:* http://freekeywords.wordtracker .com/)

7. **Wikipedia article traffic statistics:** http://stats.grok.se/. This tool can help you determine interest in a topic in Wikipedia in terms of the number of visits to that page (Figure 4.11 and 4.12). Because Wikipedia currently ranks in the top three for thousands of keywords, this can be an easy way to validate traffic volume, as compared to volumes to other traffic research tools. If an article related to a topic has very high traffic in Wikipedia, chances are there is high demand for its related keywords in Google and other search engines.

continues

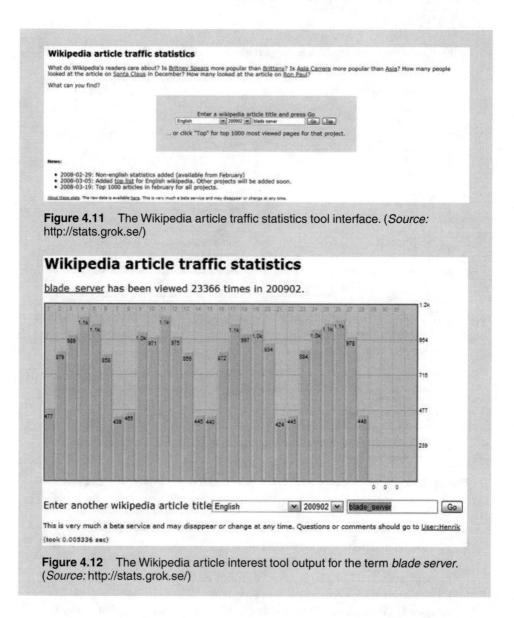

Figure 4.11   The Wikipedia article traffic statistics tool interface. (*Source:* http://stats.grok.se/)

Figure 4.12   The Wikipedia article interest tool output for the term *blade server*. (*Source:* http://stats.grok.se/)

When we consult with content teams about SEO with regard to keyword research, our clients sometimes think that keyword research tools are 100% accurate. This is a misconception, because we generally see varying results when using different tools for the same keyword. The results for each tool are based on a different sample searches and different sources. Some tools, like Wordtracker, use specific search engines. No tool can capture 100% of all Internet searches for a given keyword.

For example, the popular free Google AdWords Keyword Research tool (Figure 4.13) is really a **pay-per-click (PPC)** tool that also counts any clicks on an impression as an actual search. When Google provides approximate numbers, it draws from a variety of sources, not just the number of searches on a term in a given month. It also includes clicks on impressions, parked domain advertisements (domains registered for possible future use or to prevent competitive purchase) and searches from partner engines as well. All of these, along with the addition of robot searches, can inflate the numbers.

Figure 4.13 A Google AdWords interface. (*Source:* Google)

So with these Google results, if you divide the approximate average search volume of 14,800 per month by 30 (the number of days in month) you get around 493 searches per day. The conundrum is that you still cannot determine how many searches came from particular actions, such as clicks on impressions. What Google is measuring is more about users' interest in the keyword (in this case, *server virtualization*) than about actual searches. The search volume numbers should be used to compare various keywords.

In general, keyword research tools provide value by showing searcher interest, competition for keywords, semantically related alternatives, keyword comparisons, and seed words to use in social media for further long-tail research. We advise that you use them in conjunction with each other, because no one tool provides a complete picture of the demand, competition, and relevance for your content of a particular keyword.

Getting Started with Keyword Research

No matter what tools you use, you need to have an idea about the keywords to test out in the first place. This is a complex process involving several steps. The first step for keyword discovery is to obtain a list of so-called **seed words**. These are the usual descriptive words, also known as *themes, topics, core terms,* or *keyword clouds.* This process involves brainstorming about the main words that your target audience associates with a topic. The cloud should contain all the grammatical variations of the words, as well as all synonyms. Seed words are typically root words, from which it is relatively easy to add prefixes, suffixes, and contextual combinations of the words.

It's important to start this process with the most generic words you can think of and gradually narrow the list down until you have a manageable list to test in your tool. For example, when an IBM content team needed a list of keywords for a set of Web pages promoting environmentally friendly technologies, the team joked that it needed to start the process with the terms *earth, air, fire* and *water*—the most elementary terms in Aristotle's lexicon. Though it was a joke, it demonstrated just how broad the initial pass of possible terms and their relations needed to be. Starting with a small, broad list ensures that you won't miss any terms that might particularly connect with your target audience. You can always go back and narrow your keyword list down, but it is really hard to go back and include a whole cloud of related terms after the fact.

If it seems daunting to sit down with a content team in front of a white board and write down the most elementary words, with all their linguistic variations, the keyword tools can help. Many of them can generate all possible grammatical variations of terms, and their synonyms, from a small list. Of course, they ultimately help you determine how many users search on the keywords. They also provide insights on which terms are more competitive and which terms drive more qualified visitors. See the sidebar for a description of the four to seven tools we recommend, in order. Suffice it to say that the goal is to have a list of related keywords that will attract your targeted audience through Google. When you have your list of keywords, you then try to write one page of content for each keyword in your Web architecture. We discuss these architectural considerations in Chapter 6.

As we said, the ideal state is to have all your keywords before you write, but that is not always possible. Many search optimization efforts happen after the fact. In a sense, it is easier to do keyword research after the fact, though it might not be as effective. The reason is that there are all kinds of tools that enable you to scan your existing content for keyword frequency and develop a list of seed words from that list. Tools such as the Word Frequency Calculator (www.darylkinsman.ca/tools/wordfreq.shtml) enable you to cut and paste your existing copy into a box and generate a report on the words that appear most often. You can also exclude stop words (articles and logical connectors) or focus just on elements such as nouns or verbs. If a word appears often in an existing piece of content, it's a candidate to add to your keyword cloud.

Of course, word frequency is not the only consideration. For example, you might have a legal disclaimer on the bottom of every page that contains words completely irrelevant to the content on a page, yet a frequency counter might list them as the most frequently used words on it. Tools can help, but it typically takes human intelligence, especially from the writers and editors of the content, to develop a list of seed words from a set of existing content.

Once you have the cloud of words you want to test, you can run it through the keyword tools. Typically, you'll discover that the keywords you chose when you first published your content are not often searched on (as was the case in the case study in the sidebar). The keyword tools will generate reports that show which related words or phrases were most often searched on. Then again, you will need human intelligence to determine which words best target the desired audience while generating more traffic from search than the original words. Often, several very similar words will have similar search numbers. In that case, you make your best guess and test after the fact. It is often more important to get the content up and connect with your target audience right away than to deliberate to perfectly target your audience, and thus delay your publishing efforts. As we say at IBM, search optimization is like washing your hair: Lather, rinse, repeat.

Step-by-Step Keyword Research

This three-part graphic developed by Elliance.com shows the keyword discovery and research process in a nutshell. (Source: Elliance.com)

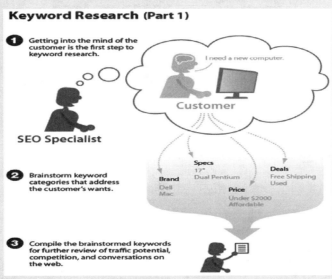

© 2007 Elliance, Inc. | elliance.com

The process of identifying the optimal keyword for a Web page can follow these simple steps:

1. Review content on the page for main or repeating themes and generate a seed list.

   a. Break down the text to surface ongoing topics and themes within your content.

   b. Review words, phrases, text structure, and patterns to help you locate semantic relationships that can lead you to finding related keywords.

continues

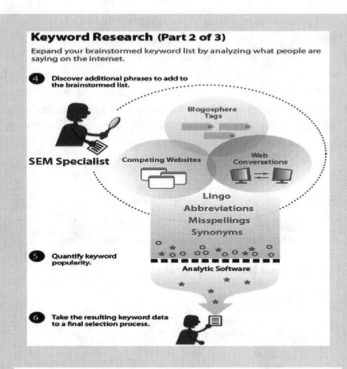

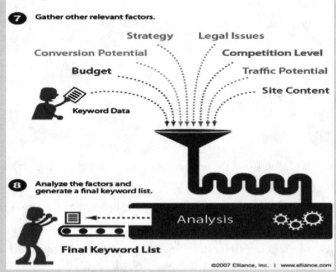

2. Use keyword research tools to help you generate more fully defined keyword candidates from your seed list. These steps will help you further understand what words people really use and what words are actually driving people to the site.

   a. Find related terms. Stemming those words and associated text can help vary and balance your content to help avoid overuse or misuse of keywords.

   b. Use a variety of tools to allow for a more comprehensive set of keyword recommendations. We will go over some available tools below.

3. Review competition for keywords (in search engines).

   a. Determine the search volume and competition for the keywords through tools such as Google AdWords, the Keyword Discovery Tool, or other available tools.

   b. Research each keyword candidate to discover keyword variations, number of searches, and competition for the keyword.

   You can never research your competition enough. Actually, it's an opportunity to learn from other approaches, with the caveat that competitive pages may not necessarily be well optimized. This part of the exercise allows you to review what is being done elsewhere to get additional ideas for your site.

4. You are now at the point where you can productively brainstorm with your client by sharing analysis, research, and keyword recommendations. Prioritize your keyword candidate list in order:

   a. High: The keyword is a close match to your site's content and is very popular or moderately popular or has a high conversion rate.

   b. Medium: The keyword is a close match to your site and is somewhat popular, with acceptable conversion rates.

   c. Low: The keyword is a close match to your site and has enough searches to be worth a paid placement bid—buying keywords to appear at the top or right column in Google results is called *paid placement*—but is not worthy of organic search optimization. It may have too much competition for organic optimization.

5. Select keywords after you have done all competitive research and keyword discovery with available free and/or paid tools.

Optimizing Web Pages with Your Keywords

Google sends **crawlers** or **spiders** through the Web to find content that might be relevant to its users. These are simply programs that scan pages and return information about pages back to Google. Based on this information, Google then places the pages into its index. The index listing for a piece of content contains the information about the page that the crawler gathered, which helps the algorithm rank the page against others on the Web for the same keywords.

Optimizing pages for a given keyword is about providing the information the Google crawler is looking for in an efficient way. If the crawler has to work hard to find the information it's seeking, it might not capture the information you want it to, and the content that ends up in Google will have an incomplete index entry. For example, if a page includes a Flash experience or a lot of JavaScript, the crawler might not capture all its content, and the page will not rank well. (For this reason, we recommend HTML or XML pages, with limited JavaScript, and Flash modules that sit like graphics files in the HTML or XML.) Without a complete index entry, the algorithm will not rank the page as highly as it would with a complete one. Optimizing a page is about making sure that the content on the page is structured for easy crawling and accurate indexing.

One of the reasons Google does a better job than any other search engine is the tuning of its crawler. Crawlers scan certain elements on a page to determine relevance. They look for parts of the code, in addition to the body copy. They especially look for the `<title>` tag, which is the text that appears at the top bar of a browser window on the left (number 1 in Figure 4.14). They also look for the `<h1>` tag or heading for a page (number 2 in Figure 4.14). Then they scan the body copy on a page (number 3 in Figure 4.14). And they look for links. This is very similar to the way users scan a page before determining whether or not to engage with its content. So tuning your pages for Google's crawler will also help you tune your pages for your users.

The Google crawler scans the text in the source code for a page. At IBM, when we audit pages, we select `View > Source` from the browser menu and try to emulate the crawler by searching for the `<title>` tag, `<h1>` tag, and placement of the body copy and the links. Then we try to ensure that the chosen keyword appears in those places. That's easy enough for the `<title>` tag and `<h1>` tag. But ensuring this for body copy can get a little tricky. Because we are mostly concerned about how to write for the Web, as opposed to how to code pages for the Web, we will focus on the body copy.

The most important aspect of writing body copy is ensuring that it contains the keywords that appear in the `<title>` tag. The next most important is the `<h1>` tag. In the example in Figure 4.14, the keyword is *Product Lifecycle Management (PLM)*. Beyond that simple requirement, there are a variety of techniques you can use to optimize your body copy.

Figure 4.14 The ibm.com Product Lifecycle Management page. Item number 1 is how the browser displays the `<title>` tag. Item number 2 is how the browser displays the `<H1>` tag or heading. Item number 3 is how the browser displays the body copy. The crawler scans these three elements, first looking for keywords and their derivatives. Note that this page was later optimized. It is used here as an example of how to improve your pages. (*Source:* IBM Corp.)

Ensure that Google pulls the text you want it to display in its **SERP** (the search engine results page, which it shows when it completes a search). This is the 150 characters of text that Google publishes to users between the title and the URL on the SERP (see Figure 4.15). There are two ways to do this. You can type exactly what you want into the `<meta content="description">` tag, or you can focus on the first 150 words of the body copy. The easier of the two is to put it into the `<meta content="description">` tag, because this gives you some freedom to write a first sentence that is more compelling for humans in your body copy. But, generally speaking, if your first sentence is identical to the 150-character snippet on the SERP, it's good enough. If it's compelling enough to get a user to click through from the SERP, it's compelling enough to put in the first sentence of your body copy.

IBM - **Smarter Planet** - United States - 5 visits - Aug 23
Computing advances allow us to add a layer of intelligence to the basic processes that run our
world: roads, water, power. Now, we can make our **planet** ...
www.ibm.com/innovation/ - Cached - Similar - 💬 ⊞ ✕

A Smarter Planet
Sep 25, 2009 ... Building a **Smarter Planet** is a blog intended to provide readers with thought-
provoking content and a place to talk about the issues raised within the ...
Smart Banking - Smarter Cities - George Faulkner
asmarterplanet.com/ - Cached - Similar - 💬 ⊞ ✕

The case for health reform: New video and podcast | A **Smarter Planet**
Feb 26, 2009 ... It doesn't come as a surprise to anybody that our health systems are in need
of significant reform. Part of that reform is digitizing ...
asmarterplanet.com/.../the-case-for-health-reform-new-video-and-podcast.html -
Cached - Similar - 💬 ⊞ ✕

Figure 4.15   Three listings on Google's SERP for the keyword Smarter Planet. In the first
two cases, the `<meta content="description">` tag specifies the copy we want to
portray to the target audience to get them to click through. In the third case, Google pulls
the first 150 characters of the body copy. (*Source:* www.google.com)

Beyond what you want to display on the SERP, you can do a lot of things with the
body copy to enhance its position in search engines for your keywords. We will focus on
the most important tactics in this section: spelling out acronyms, pumping up keyword density, ensuring keyword proximity, stemming verbs, using synonyms and other related
words, using descriptive link text, and bolding for emphasis.

- **Spelling out acronyms:** In the example in Figure 4.14. the term *Product Lifecycle Management* is abbreviated *PLM*. In print, the common style for acronyms
  and other abbreviations is to spell them out on first reference and never spell
  them out again. This is not a good tactic for the Web. The crawler needs to see the
  full unabbreviated form of the keyword in all three primary locations. So, for
  example, the body copy in Figure 4.14 starts with the abbreviated form. That's a
  no-no. It should start by spelling out *Product Lifecycle Management (PLM)*. It
  can use the abbreviated form in the body copy afterwards. But unlike in print, the
  abbreviated form should be used only when readability is not affected. Use the
  spelled-out form as often as possible. That's what the crawler is looking for.
  That's one action item we took when we later optimized that page.

- **Pumping up keyword density:** After the first sentence, ideally, *between 2 and 4
  percent* of your body copy should contain the keyword in your `<title>` and
  `<H1>` tags. This might seem absurd to writers accustomed to using the entire lexicon available to them to engage the reader. But it is a goal to strive for in Web
  copy writing. There are ways of pumping up keyword density without overwhelming the reader with repetitive language. The strict rule in the print world
  that dictates that you should find alternative words if you see the same word

twice in a short span of text does not apply on the Web, especially when it comes
to keywords. That said, you don't want to go over the 4 percent rule, lest you
invoke the dreaded spam algorithm that Google uses to weed out blatant attempts
to trick it into driving traffic to irrelevant content for the sake of ad dollars.

- **Ensuring keyword proximity:** All things considered, *if your keyword contains
  multiple words,* the closer the *words* are in proximity, the easier it is for the
  crawler to associate them. For example, if the above body copy contained the
  phrase ***managing*** *your **product lifecycles,*** the crawler would have an easier time
  making the association with the keyword than if it contained the phrase *it is
  important to **manage** the **lifecycle** of the **products** in your portfolio.* The words
  need not be in the same order, or even adjacent to each other, for the crawler to
  associate them with the keywords in the `<title>` and `<h1>` tags. But the
  closer the better.

- **Stemming:** This is the use of alternative grammatical forms of words. For
  example, from *stem* you could have *stem, stemmed, stemming, stems,* etc.
  Because users will enter keywords in many different forms, you have a better
  chance of getting search results if you make it a point to stem your verbs in your
  body copy. Of course, you don't want to mix tenses. But you can use the *gerund*
  (*stemming*) and the *present perfect (stems)* form in the same paragraph, for
  example. Another reason to stem is that it enables you to gain more keyword density without replicating the same words over and over again. And it is relatively
  easy to mix the different *forms of nouns,* as in Figure 4.16, to use adjectives in
  adverbial phrases, and to apply other similar strategies.

- **Using synonyms and other related words:** When you do your initial keyword
  research, you will develop your seed words, then from that you will develop a
  keyword cloud of related words from your set of seed words. Don't discard the
  keyword cloud after you choose your keywords. This is a handy tool to use as
  you write. For every sentence in the English language, there are something like
  thirty alternative ways of expressing the same thing with different related words.
  Chances are, your audience will use the entire range of these expressions, especially considering audience diversity. The more of these you can capture by using
  the entire keyword cloud, the better your search results will be.

- **Using descriptive link text:** Because the crawler doesn't just look at the body
  copy, but especially focuses on links, it is important that your links be as descriptive as your body text. Don't just replicate the heading of the site to which you're
  linking: Describe the site, preferably with the keywords in your `<title>` and
  `<h1>` tags. And don't just use generic links like *Learn more* or *Download the
  PDF.* Use the keywords of the page or media piece to which you are linking.

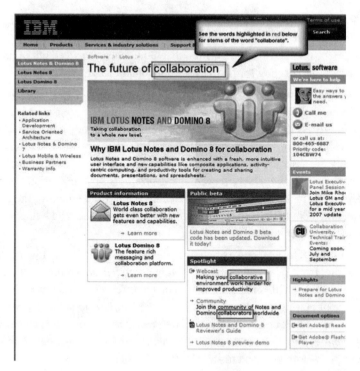

Figure 4.16   This example from the IBM site shows stemming with the use of collaboration, collaborative, and collaborators on the page. (*Source:* IBM Corp.)

- **Bolding for emphasis:** Web users' eyes tend to cue into bullet points, bolding, and other ways of emphasizing text. If you have the opportunity to do this with your keywords, it's a good practice. It's good for the crawler and for the user who comes to your site from Google using those keywords. You are less likely to get bounce and more likely to get engagement if it is easy for the user to understand the relevance of your page in a few seconds of scanning.

Many site owners mistakenly believe that ranking high for any term closely related to the content of their page will produce an influx of targeted visitors. Although this may get you more traffic, these high rankings will not always drive *qualified* visitors to your site or page. Your goal is to find keywords that are *relevant to your audience*. That means using the words and phrases common to your target audience in your body copy. The above techniques can help you hedge your bets that your diverse audience will use one form or another of the keywords in your cloud, which you developed from your seed words.

In Chapter 5, we will explain how to discover and use not only the *keyword phrases* that your target audience uses, but their *exact language*. This involves sophisticated long-tail research and social media mining tactics. Wherever feasible, it's important to learn as much as possible about your target audience, especially the words and phrases that they use in search and social media contexts. Because Web content is never finished and testing is an integral part of the publishing process, your efforts can start with search and mature into social media as time and resources permit.

Summary

The search-first Web writing methodology is a radical departure from print writing, where you *passively* attract readers interested in your books and articles. In Web writing, you *actively* attract an audience that is more likely to find your content relevant if it is written for them with the building blocks of Web content—*keywords*. This chapter describes the tactics at the core of the search-first writing methodology. The following insights are important to understanding how to put the search-first methodology into practice.

- Define your target audience according to the words and phrases they are likely to enter into Google.
- Research the keywords most often used in Google search queries to maximize the volume of traffic to your pages, while minimizing bounce rates.
- Write your content only after you have done a thorough analysis of how to target your audience with the keywords that your research suggests.
- Implement your keyword research into your writing by ensuring keyword density, proximity, word stemming, and using related words, synonyms, and descriptive link text.
- Measure the effectiveness of your first efforts with an eye toward republishing your content, to reduce bounce rates and improve engagement.
- Continually refine your language to better engage your target audience with relevant content.

International Keyword Research

International keyword research, also referred to as **multilingual keyword research**, can be a complex task. Here's why. You have to define whether the language usage is for international (universal), local (specific targeted country) or regional (geographic areas such as Latin America) areas. You must also carefully consider idioms and cultural distinctions, along with "sociological, contextual and intrinsic aspects of the language," as mentioned at the Spanish speaking SEO report (http://www.spanishseo.org/tips-for-multilingual-keyword-research/).

continues

Although keyword research tools can help you, it is important to engage native speakers early within your process of compiling a seed list. It is difficult to conduct sufficiently thorough keyword research in a second language unless one understands and speaks that language. That person should also be familiar with your products and/or niche.

Very few of the available keyword research tools conduct multiple language searches. If you search for terms in Simplified Chinese with a tool that doesn't support the required encoding (the most popular variety of which is **UTF-8,** a representation of the **Unicode** character set), all you would see is indecipherable characters. For example, the Japanese text 情報資源の戦略的有効活用・最適化 would render as 口口口口口口口 rather than as the proper UTF-8 characters.

For more information about Unicode, see the Unicode Consortium page: http://unicode.org/standard/WhatIsUnicode.html.

One seemingly useful tool might be **automatic translation,** also known as **machine translation.** However, it falls short of providing adequate translation interpretation. Automatic translation tools all do more or less literal translations, but they don't understand the meaning of the text within its context. Therefore, the resulting terms will rarely be appropriate and can be highly misleading. A simple example of this is the UK word *flat*, which as a noun typically means an apartment or living space, whereas in the U.S., it typically means a deflated tire or level field. Another example is when some languages combine multiple terms into one word. In German, *computer mouse* becomes *Computermaus,* but most German speakers refer to this computer device as a *Maus.*

There are also difficulties in the translations of English words. There are many linguistic issues owing to the various meanings of words and to cultural differences. Because of these, many keyword research tools do not provide meaningful, inflected permutations. Getting good translations of English terms is not as easy as it would seem.

As noted by Marios Alexandrou,[1] some automated translation tools, such as Alta Vista's Babel Fish, "are prone to do literal translations rather than ones that match how people actually speak." Even numbers can be a problem. Some languages only have different words for *one, two, three* and *many*. And for singulars and plurals, there are stemming differences and problems in translation throughout all countries and languages.

There are also gender differences. As you've probably experienced before, words in many Romance languages have gender, and this affects the articles used with them. In Spanish, for example, gender articles are sometimes included in search keywords, and sometimes not, depending on the context. When searching for the word *servi-*

---

1. See www.allthingssem.com/international-seo-keyword-research/.

dores (servers), a Spanish speaker might type either `servidores` or `los servi-`
`dores` when searching for a phrase such as *los servidores de los años 1990* (*the*
servers that existed in the 1990s).

To make things even more interesting, gender articles can differ between lan-
guage, such as *el sol* (*the sun* in Spanish, <u>masculine</u>) versus *Die Sonne* (*the sun* in
German, <u>feminine</u>). This would just be a case of ensuring accurate translation from
English.

You also need to consider, what do you translate, and what do you not translate?
What should be translated depends on the country, language, and audience. You need
to ask yourself what people look for in translations, both in English and in other languages. The key in terms of search may be to find what users are primarily looking
for. This can be a problem because translators are often faced with two options:

1. Using the term from the original language, and possibly needing to explain it (but
   also increasing the reader's knowledge). For example, the term *data warehouse*
   sometimes is used in Spanish technical texts, but it may need explanation the first
   time it appears.

2. Simply translating or explaining the term, making it easier for the reader but not
   increasing his or her knowledge. If a consistent translation is used (such as the
   Spanish *infraestructura* for *infrastructure*), this can work well. But if a word
   has more than one acceptable translation, or can only be explained, this makes
   keyword optimization harder.

The key in terms of search may be to find for sure what users are primarily looking for.

Another problem involves the way that words "migrate" from one language to
another. Would Chinese words find their way into Japanese, or the other way around?
Some languages will have some words in common. Japanese and Chinese for example,
would produce similar results for many one-word or two-word search items. But in
Japanese, once grammar, punctuation, or foreign words are introduced, it will be
completely distinct from Chinese.

Fortunately, with the majority of languages, it is quite possible that any interna-
tionally accepted words would be searched for in English, surrounded by the grammar of the original language. In our experience, the Web has increased even further
the amount of borrowed English words in other languages. For example, words like
login, Facebook, server, and *database*, which come from English, have reached
wide usage in other languages. So, some well-known product or brand names such as
Windows or *Facebook* shouldn't be translated, since most people will still refer to
their original names in English.

Some languages have more synonyms than others, which can cause problems.
Local knowledge of search and industry terms would be key in selecting which of sev-

continues

eral synonyms to allocate with higher priority. For example, for the term *drink*, we may have more than one term in some languages, but one single term in others:

English: Drink, beverage

Spanish: Bebida, algo de tomar, trago, gaseosa, copa

German: Getränk

Japanese: 飲み物

Selecting someone in-country who is aware of the most commonly used terms in daily conversation might be a good way to tackle which keywords are best to include where.

So when you begin your international keyword research, think about the following.

- Define your language objectives.

- Involve a native speaker experienced with your company's product or niche market.

- Have an awareness/understanding that not all keyword tools are equal and some may not properly provide useful multilingual keyword research. Consider having your terms professionally translated where possible.

- Conduct market research where possible to determine who your local competitors are and what terms they are using.

- Get the keywords *before* you create the content. A more successful approach would be to come up with keywords from scratch—think of what the right keywords would be for someone who speaks another language, rather than just taking the English and forcing a translation. What term should be used, versus what would a translation say? You need to discern if the terms are reflective of the searcher's queries and local marketplace.

- Engage your customers to find out how they came to your site, and what terms and search engines they used. Information from native speakers in your foreign markets can be the most insightful.

Below are some tools that work well for international keyword research.

- Google AdWords tool: https://adwords.google.com/select/KeywordToolExternal

- Google Traffic Estimator: https://adwords.google.com/select/TrafficEstimatorSandbox

CHAPTER 5

Engaging with Your Web Visitors through More Targeted Search Referrals

On the Web, you do not address a generic passive audience; you engage a defined active one. That engagement starts with attracting a targeted audience with keywords, as we explained in the previous chapter. But it doesn't end there. Search engines can help you attract a targeted audience, but once you get that audience on your site, you need to engage them with compelling links. This chapter is about helping visitors understand how to engage with your content, so they can use it to find what they need.

Making your audience engage deeply with your content has two main components. The first is a common consideration for all writing, which is especially important in Web writing: **purpose.** The most important thing about purpose is that content can be relevant to an audience in one visit and not in the next. Why? Because your visitors' information-related needs change as they consume it. Content that readers find redundant is also irrelevant to them. Helping users find fresh content on topics of interest is both a challenge and an opportunity for Web publishers. This is another way that Web publishing differs from print. Print publications are complete. They either serve the intended purpose or they do not. But Web sites are always incomplete: If you find that your pages can do a better job of serving their intended purposes, you can and should change them.

Purpose is only the most important variable that affects how to create relevant experiences for Web audiences. As you know, natural language is quite complex, involving many other variables that affect relevance. You can simplify the problem by focusing on keywords, but you don't want to oversimplify it in the process. We can help you understand how keywords and phrases affect the overall content of your pages, so that your site can engage visitors more deeply. The second half of this chapter shows how you can engage more deeply with your audience's use of language. These methods include knowing their long-tail keyword habits in their search behavior, and discovering your audience's writing and tagging habits in social media. If you know your audience at a deeper level, you can more deeply engage with them, by using *their* language when you write.

Using Page Purpose to Engage with Your Audience

Consider the following scenario. A user searches on an IBM product name and lands on an ibm.com marketing page for that product. The user already owns the product, but wants to find support pages for it. So even though the page's topic is relevant to the visitor's search query, the page itself is not. Why? Because the page's purpose did not match the user's interests. In fact, ibm.com receives many "Rate This Page" surveys in which people describe precisely this experience, essentially saying "Stop selling me a product I already own!" Our company's marketing department works very hard to optimize its pages for search and garners the majority of the search visits for product names. It does this even though we know that 60 percent of ibm.com visitors are looking for support for products they already own.

This illustrates the importance of including a page's purpose in its keywords. This is important for different functional groups, such as marketing and support. But it's also important within individual functional groups. For example, on a page that falls under marketing's responsibility, one visitor might want to learn *how to solve a particular problem* with IBM technology, while another wants to look at *what technology offerings might help solve the problem*. In IBM we call the first purpose **awareness** and the second one **consideration**. Awareness pages tend to be more relevant for visitors who are trying to solve a problem, while consideration pages tend to be more relevant for those who want to compare and contrast potential solutions to a problem.

Some pages that are relevant to the same keywords are designed to help visitors with different purposes consume the same content. These generic landing pages are useful, but you only need a few of them. Most of your content will need to have a basic defined purpose for each page. To avoid negative user experiences like those shown in some of IBM's user surveys, you'll need to develop content that makes its purpose explicit in the title tag, as well as elsewhere on the page.

In some fields, this process is called **task analysis**—a term borrowed from software engineering—in which you develop **use cases** and make sure your pages accommodate most of them. A *use case* is a scenario in which a user experience (fictional or otherwise) is described. Most pages have several use cases; entire sites might have more use cases than can be enumerated. You can never anticipate your visitors' every move. But, as we have said repeatedly, the beauty of the Web is that you can adjust your pages for the users who come to them. So even if you do not anticipate all the paths your visitors might take, you can follow their movements and make it easier on them as time goes on, by adjusting your experiences to suit their needs.

Though task analysis can help you engage with your visitors after they come to your pages, you can also precondition them by helping them land directly on the pages relevant to their tasks when they come from search engines. Along with having keywords that describe each page's *topic*, be sure to include each page's *purpose* in the keywords in its title tag, heading, and URL. The tasks that we use in marketing contexts (which we elaborate on in the sidebar) are borrowed from the sales cycle, including awareness and consideration. For example, perhaps you have one base keyword phrase, say *Service Oriented Architecture*. You should then add a *purpose* to each page's title tag, such as *Service Oriented Architecture: Learn About* and *Service Oriented Architecture: Compare Products.*

Ways to Think of Purpose

A user might be interested in *content* related to a keyword, but not the *purpose* of the content with that keyword in it. Purposes come in different flavors. A common way that we think about page purpose at IBM involves where a user is in the sales cycle:

- **Awareness:** Users initially come to the site to become aware of what IBM offers in a technology category; here, they need generic information about how the technology category solves business problems.

- **Interest:** After becoming more aware of the issues involved with applying technology to a business problem, some users will decide not to pursue it further. Those who continue to explore the issues with deeper engagement into our content are therefore showing interest in a possible purchase. Here, they need high-level information about how IBM offerings might solve the business problem.

- **Consideration:** Users then seek advice on their options as they consider purchasing an offering that helps solve the problem. Here, they need detailed information that differentiates the various options by features, costs, benefits, and expected return on investment.

- **Purchase:** If they enter the sales cycle, users need information on whom to contact, what financing and other offers are available, and how to take advantage of those offers.

- **Support:** Customers often need information on how to set up, use, optimize, and integrate the products they buy into a whole IT infrastructure.

- **Service:** Customers sometimes need information about how to get their products fixed or extended to perform better in their changing IT environments.

In Figure 5.1, borrowed from the authors' IBM SEO marketing course, we show that keyword use changes at each stage of the buying cycle. Although the *root* keywords remain relevant at all stages, *specific* keyword phrases change, depending on users' need for information.

A user might come to your site from a search engine for any of the reasons discussed above (and others as well). One common complaint when customers come to a site by searching on a product name is that they land on a page that deals with *consideration* when they want *support information*, or on a *support page* when they just want to *learn the high level concepts* related to a technology category.

continues

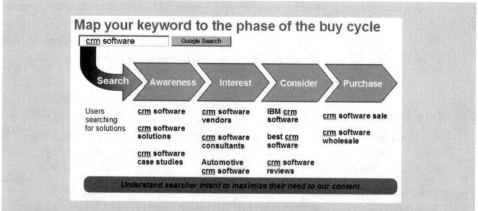

Figure 5.1   A typical hierarchy of keywords based on page purposes. (*Source:* IBM's *Organic Search Authoring Basics* course)

Suppose your site promotes smarter healthcare and has two stories about patient information management. One page could be about the generic concepts (such as defining the problem or describing the solutions at a high level). Here, users' engagement is directed to information that gives them *awareness*. Other pages on the site might direct users to take action to find the particular solutions that matter to them. In particular, you might have a section for hospital administrators to evaluate products. This would be at the level of *consideration*.

Even when coming to pages with the same content topics, visitors may have a wide variety of purposes and tasks in mind. We can't say this too often: The way to differentiate these pages for Google users is to state each page's purpose clearly in the title tag, heading, URL, and abstract. In the abstract, tell users what you want them to do when they get to your page. In the above example, the keyword phrase might be *medical information management.* Perhaps that is also what you use in the awareness-level page. But in the consideration-level pages, you can add purpose qualifiers. For example, the lower-level pages might have the keyword phrases *medical information management—evaluating patient privacy solutions,* or *medical information management—evaluating portable data solutions.* And you could have a number of pages with different verbs in them, like *purchasing, supporting, extending,* and *integrating.* If portions of your target audience are interested in these different purposes, consider building such pages a click or two off from the generic landing page.

You can also precondition users by making sure that the page purpose is in the metadescription (`<meta content="description">`) in your page code. This will end up in the short description or snippet that search engines display in the search engine results page (SERP). Users who read this snippet will have a better idea of the page purpose before they land on your page from Google or other search engines.

We will discuss how to build site architectures using keywords as each page's reason for being in Chapter 6. Considering purpose through task analysis is one of the prime ways to create an engaging site architecture. But to build a complete site that engages your audience at a deep level and keeps them coming back again and again in search of relevant content, you need to look deeper than just purpose. You must explore the depths of your audience's vocabulary: not just their keywords in isolation, but their keyword clouds, and the myriad grammatical constructions they could use to combine keywords into meaningful sentences.

Going beyond Mere Keywords to Determine Relevance for an Audience

In the previous chapter, we assumed for the moment that all you know about your audience on the Web is that they came to your page from Google using a keyword string. But you often can know more than that. If you develop a deeper understanding of the language your visitors use—not just vocabulary, but also phraseology—you can engage more deeply with them. The rest of this chapter is about learning about your audience's language use, in a way made possible only on the Web: through participating in their favorite social media sites.

A user can find the content on a page (with the same keywords) relevant one week and irrelevant the next. You might ask: How can this happen? If keyword usage determines relevance, how can attracting users to your pages though keywords sometimes drive them to irrelevant information? Well, language is a lot more complex than a simple matching algorithm between keywords and users. If it were that simple, Web writing and editing would be a matter for technology and not humans. But humans are needed to make good content decisions based on a variety of variables, including keyword usage.

What variables other than purpose affect whether content is relevant? One key variable is **content freshness**. All things considered, content that is up to date will be more relevant to users than stale content. But this is not an either/or proposition. There are degrees of content freshness. Also, not all content needs to be fresh. The relevance of news falls off quickly after it is published. On the other hand, product specifications retain freshness for a long time. Users have different expectations of freshness for different types of content. A podcast is expected to be recent, whereas certain white papers are **evergreen**, meaning that they stay fresh indefinitely. Fortunately, it is not hard to find out your users' expectations of freshness for each content type. You can even set up systems that tell you when a piece of content has expired and automatically take it down.

There are many more variables that affect relevance than we have space to enumerate. That is for linguists to deal with, rather than writing instructors. But we can point you to a few additional ways to learn how your audience phrases their needs, so you can better meet those needs with relevant content. You can do more sophisticated long-tail keyword research, using what we know about how search engines determine relevance for longer queries. And you can learn more about how your audience writes and responds in social media settings. These two tactics are the subject of the rest of this chapter.

Using the Power of the Web to Better Understand Your Audience

In the last chapter, we assumed for the sake of simplicity that all you know about your audience is that they came to your site by searching on keywords. That simplifying assumption was needed to help you understand the level of knowledge this gives you, and to help you write your content for initial publication. However, after you publish your content, you will need to learn a lot more about your audience. You can do this through metrics tools and site surveys that can help you adjust your content to serve your audience's needs better.

One method of understanding your audience is to set up surveys. One survey at ibm.com is "Rate This Page." This is a module that content owners can place on their pages to ask direct questions of their readers. IBM currently has three such surveys:

- **The Basic module.** This asks users if the page helped them achieve their goals and lets them comment on the page. This is especially good for transactional pages without much content.

- **The Writing Quality module.** This asks a series of questions about how clear and concise the writing on the page is. It also has a comment field.

- **The Relevance module.** This asks users how relevant the content is to them. It also asks them to specify their job role and includes an open comment field.

Even if only a small percentage of your visitors fill out the survey, these modules can help you get very good feedback about how well your content meets its users' needs.

Because audiences have a wide variety of demographics and needs, surveys can't cover all of them. Even at their best, they only give you audience understanding *after the fact*. But it is always better to know more about your target audience *before you write for them*. So, you should always perform previous audience analysis. Here are some ways you can do so.

Pre-Publishing Audience Analysis:

1. **Conduct field studies** or focus groups to get a sense of actual user sentiment.

2. **Conduct readership studies** with representative audience members to determine desired future content.

3. **Mine social media sites** such as communities and forums to understand what users care about. You can understand your audience's interests and needs by posting questions to these sites.

4. **Listen to blog posts and message board threads.** Subscribe to their RSS feeds to look for topic patterns. If your referrer is from a blog, see if there is a blogroll that will identify his or her interests. Doing these things will give you a flavor of what is currently popular.

5. **Establish accounts in microblogging sites like Twitter** to interact with potential audience members. You can use them to monitor the buzz about your content. Also, subscribe to RSS feeds and respond to Tweets by providing pertinent information when the opportunity arises.

6. **Participate in virtual worlds** like Second Life to ask questions of individuals who visit your organization's pages.

Post-Publishing Audience Analysis:

1. **Use the reverse IP look-up function,** which allows you to find where your users are coming from (by categories such as company, organization, and service provider).

2. **Analyze referring URL data** to identify which social media sites your customers participate in. This could provide information on demographics and interests.

3. **Analyze site traffic to show trends** and identify gaps. Identify which pages receive no traffic and take them down or modify them.

4. **Analyze engagement to see which links are the most and least popular.** Promote the popular links and take down those with no clicks.

5. **Watch RSS feed popularity.** If users are subscribing to content, it demonstrates a lot of interest in it.

6. **Conduct polls** to gauge customer interest and issues. Be sure to change your questions frequently.

7. **Capture aggregate personalization information,** which can provide further demographics about your users.

8. **Conduct Customer Relationship Management (CRM) analysis** for additional insight into your users' demographics and behavior.

continues

9. **Perform competitive analysis,** which allows you to see products and services being added or dropped by your competitors.

The beauty of the Web is the speed with which you can adjust your content to better meet user needs. If your best guess is off the mark, try something else and test again. Unlike print, Web publishing is not finished when the content is published. It is an ongoing, iterative process to tune published content to better meet visitors' needs.

Using Keyword Research to Optimize for Long Tails

What are long-tail keywords? They are not necessarily longer strings of keywords, as you might think. The term *The Long Tail* was coined by *Wired* magazine's editor Chris Anderson in an article in 2004 (and elaborated in 2006 in his book by the same name). The Long Tail is a marketing concept in which companies sell small volumes of hard-to-find items to high volumes of diverse customers. One example of this model is Etsy.com, a cooperative site for people who create niche crafts such as jewelry. This is in contrast to a company that sells high volumes of just a few popular items, as Dell does. The Long Tail actually refers to the demographics of people with highly specialized, diverse needs—Etsy.com visitors, for example. The concept has been extended to keywords. **Long-tail keywords** are like hard-to find items—longer key phrases that users take the trouble to type in when they want to find something quite specific. This is in contrast to popular search words, which are highly coveted by marketers because they will draw high volumes from a relatively narrow demographic.

So far we have helped you optimize for conventional high-demand terms. This section is about capturing the long-tail demographic—diverse audiences who have unique interests in your content. This is yet another way in which Web publishing differs radically from print. In the print world, you don't get a book deal unless the publisher is convinced that the book will sell in relatively high volumes. Magazines go out of business unless the readership is large enough for advertisers to want to buy ads. On the Web, Etsy.com is an example of a very successful model. Any individual page on that site might only get ten visits per month. But the sheer volume of pages, and the depth of engagement by its users, enable Etsy.com to make money and continue to serve its constituents.

From a keyword perspective, long-tail keywords are basically an expansion of a core, generic, high-volume keyword phrase. These expansions typically include numerous combinations and permutations of high-volume keywords and their associated or relevant phrases. But they need not be longer than the original high-volume keyword. They can just be unique ways of phrasing variations of it.

According to doshdosh.com (www.doshdosh.com/how-to-target-long-tail-keywords -increase-search-traffic/), these long-tail keywords tend to be much more targeted than general or main keyword topics because they literally embody a visitor's need for specific information. Taken individually, these phrases are unlikely to account for a large number of searches. But taken as a whole, they can provide significant qualified traffic. The main advantages to optimizing pages for long-tail keywords are increased visibility and better audience targeting. Even though individual long-tail keywords do not have high demand in Google—since few people actually search on them—they produce a lot of traffic, because there are so many of them. Long-tail keywords tend to help with targeting because visitors who use such specific search phrases tend to be looking for exactly what they will find through long-tail searches.

According to Aaron Wall of SEO Book (see www.seobook.com/archives/000657 .shtml), by conducting a careful analysis of Google results and ranking pages, you can see how semantics plays into Google's ranking algorithm. The following italicized passage, which gives some of Wall's most important ideas, is taken directly from the seobook.com page mentioned above.

Nonetheless, it is overtly obvious to anyone who studies search relevancy algorithms by watching the results and ranking pages that the following are true for Google:

- *Search engines such as Google do try to figure out phrase relationships when processing queries, improving the rankings of pages with related phrases even if those pages are not focused on the target term*

- *Pages that are too focused on one phrase tend to rank worse than one would expect (sometimes even being filtered out for what some SEOs call being over-optimized)*

- *Pages that are focused on a wider net of related keywords tend to have more stable rankings for the core keyword and rank for a wider net of keywords*

When Wall speaks of "a wider net of keywords" What he means by this is capturing long-tail keyword combinations. Some pages have so little copy that it is very difficult to optimize them for anything but the chosen keywords. We recommend a minimum of 300 words on a page, which allows you to write about your topic in greater depth. This will give you more opportunities to use different word combinations and grammatical constructions related to the same topic. But don't be redundant just to get multiple long-tail combinations into your copy. And don't skimp on copy just because you just want to satisfy the scanners in your audience. There are ways of convincing scanners to read. Scanning and reading are not mutually exclusive. True, Web users tend to scan before determining if a page is worth their time. But once they determine that they want to read it, they'll read between 300 and 500 words. Make sure that you give scanners the contextual cues they need, such as bolded words and multiple headings that include keywords, but don't short change the readers either. If you satisfy both types of visitors, you'll have a better chance of capturing traffic from long-tail demographics.

In our own work optimizing pages for ibm.com, we encounter the following scenario over and over. We look for relatively high-demand keywords with relatively low

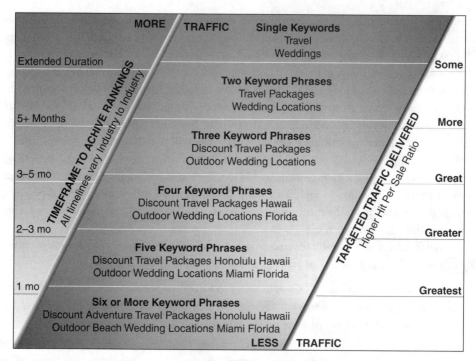

Figure 5.2   The long-tail keyword time to market and targeted traffic matrix. (*Source:* deGeyter 2008)

competition. Then we optimize pages with the keywords we chose. Our traffic to those pages might go up exponentially, but this increase is not clearly linked to the keywords we chose. We might not rank well for those words because of higher competition—it takes time to build sufficient link equity to rank well for terms with a lot of competition. But nonetheless, we get good search referral data, because users are coming to our pages from long-tail variations of keywords we chose. The reason is that in addition to optimizing for our chosen keywords, we also optimize for several related strings of words. Some of this happens naturally: Good writers tend to vary their usage patterns with the same root words to break up the monotony. But some of it is planned: We expect writers to consciously stem verb forms, to use variations of the same noun, to use synonyms, and to try to use keywords in different parts of speech. All of these writing practices cater to searchers who come to your site using long-tail keywords. The good news is that people who use long-tail searches are more apt to find your content relevant to them and are less apt to bounce off your page.

According to Stoney deGeyter (2008), a leading expert on keyword research and selection from Pole Position Marketing, Web writers should focus on word strings two to four words long when trying to target their audience through long-tail keywords: "In general, terms with two to four words are the best. With two to four words, each search term can be both descriptive and specific. If a specific term is typed into the search engine and your site appears, the searcher knows you have precisely what they are looking for." (See Figure 5.2.)

When it comes to keyword usage, the goal is to find the right combination of words to attract a more targeted audience and to engage them with the phrases they use to describe things. In marketing contexts, it costs money to optimize for high-demand words, especially those with a lot of competition. But if you optimize for long-tail keywords, you can get a much better return on investment with a smaller number of qualified visitors than you would with a large number of unqualified visitors coming to your site from high-demand keyword searches. And you can optimize for long-tail keywords more quickly than for

Long-Tail Search and Latent Semantic Indexing (LSI)

Today's search engines use semantic technologies, similar to **latent semantic indexing (LSI),** to determine the relevance of documents to a particular search query. LSI analyzes the frequency of words used in various relationships across a large set of documents. With this data, LSI uses statistical analysis to derive to what degree words are related, or roughly relevant to, other words.

LSI helps search engines determine what word combinations on a page are most likely to occur. This information is fed into the algorithm that scans pages for the most likely word combinations for a given topic. Understanding how search engines use LSI can help you develop pages that capture more traffic from long-tail queries.

The best way to learn which long-tail word combinations are drawing users to your site is to examine your search referral data, which you can glean from any commercial metrics program. Figure 5.3 shows a sample report of long-tail search referrals from ibm.com.

When you see how many people landed on your pages using a specific set of keywords, it gives you a sense of what your users expect when they get to your page. In some cases, their long-tail usage results in a bounce, because your page was not tuned for exactly that usage. (It is not clear that Google uses a true LSI application or something that mimics LSI. But for the present, we will refer to its LSI-like output as an LSI application.) But if your copy is tight and Google's LSI algorithm is doing its job, you should naturally rank well for long-tails. Even though long-tails have low demand—meaning that few people search on those particular items in a given time frame—the sheer volume of long-tail word combinations will result in a significant proportion of your traffic.

continues

smart grid definition	24
petaflop wiki	24
ge smart grid	24
ibm commercial	23
worlds fastest computer	23
smart grid news	23
world math	23
ibm tv ads	22
our galaxy map	22
ibm pedaflop	22
pedaflop	22
smart car	21
"smart planet"	21
maps of the universe	21

Figure 5.3   A snippet of a long-tail report. These are words we did not optimize for, but users came to our site using these words and clicking organic results.

high-demand words. This enables you to engage with your target audience almost as soon as you publish your content.

The other thing to keep in mind about long-tail keywords is that as users become more search-savvy, the trend is toward longer tails. As they learn how to zero in on relevant content through search, users form their search strings in more sophisticated ways, typically with three or four words. Recent research from Hitwise confirms this trend, as noted elsewhere by Matt McGee (see http://searchengineland.com/search-queries-getting-longer-16676).

> More than half of all search queries are at least three words long, and more than a third are four words or longer.

As users become more familiar with the use of search engines, their queries become more specific, and therefore are longer (Figure 5.4). McGee adds that

Percentage of U.S. Clicks by Number of Keywords			
Subject	Jan-08	Dec-08	Jan-08	Year-over-Year Percentage Change
1 word	20.96%	20.70%	20.29%	–3%
2 words	24.91%	24.13%	23.65%	–5%
3 words	22.03%	21.94%	21.92%	0%
4 words	14.54%	14.67%	14.89%	2%
5 words	8.20%	8.37%	8.68%	6%
6 words	4.32%	4.47%	4.65%	8%
7 words	2.23%	2.40%	2.49%	12%
8+ words	2.81%	3.31%	3.43%	22%

Note: Data is based on four-week rolling periods (ending Jan. 31, 2009; Dec. 27, 2008; and Jan. 26, 2008) from the Hitwise sample of 10 million U.S. Internet users.

Source: Hitwise, an Experian company

Figure 5.4 This chart from Hitwise shows how over time, click-throughs for longer search queries have increased. (Cited by Matt McGee at http://searchengineland.com/search-queries-getting-longer-16676)

The takeaway point here is that the so-called long-tail of search continues to get longer. As searchers get more sophisticated in how they use Google, Yahoo, Live Search, etc., it opens up more opportunities for webmasters and marketers to create content and ads that capture these longer search queries.

Two Research Tools for Long-Tail Keywords

Quintura (www.quintura.com) is a tool offered gratis for the time being (Figure 5.5). (Tools like this tend to require payment when demand increases after they are offered free of charge.) It locates popular search topics related to your keywords and supplies a cloud or visual map. Once your query is processed, words contextually related to it are displayed in the left pane of the Quintura window. The Quintura cloud or visual map shows the context of your query and the words and word combinations most closely connected with it.

continues

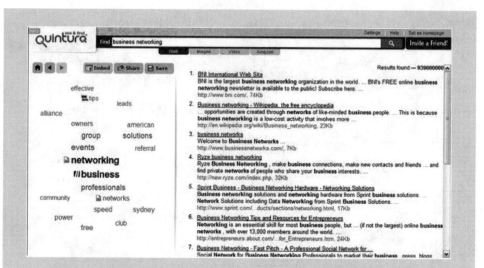

Figure 5.5   Quintura tag cloud tool. (*Source:* www.quintura.com)

Lexical FreeNet (www.lexfn.com) is another semantic relationship tool offered free of charge for the present (Figure 5.6). It lets you search for relationships between words, concepts, and people. It is a combination thesaurus, rhyming dictionary, pun generator, and concept navigator. Use it to find words that fit the needs of whatever writing endeavor you've undertaken, or just to browse concept space.

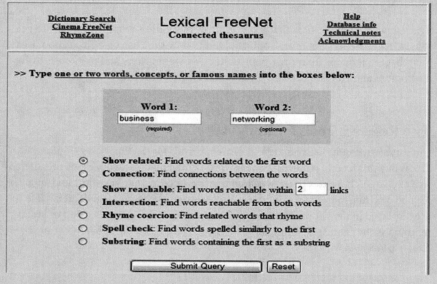

Figure 5.6   Lexical FreeNet input screen. (*Source:* www.lexfn.com)

Writing for long-tail keywords mostly follows naturally from writing good Web copy. Don't use the same constructions over and over, but vary them, using synonyms and different grammatical combinations to communicate related concepts. And don't skimp on body copy. If you understand how your audience is coming to your pages through long-tail keyword combinations, you can edit them to include the combinations that your audience enters into search queries. This helps you to grow a highly targeted audience.

Using Social Media to Enhance Your Audience Understanding

You can define the audience you want to attract by using the combination of research methods outlined in the sidebar "Using the Power of the Web to Better Understand Your Audience." But that definition never completely captures the audience that comes to your site and finds your content relevant. After you publish your content, people will come to your site who you never expected would find your content relevant. How do you get to know these folks better? We recommend letting your audience contribute to your site by commenting on your content. You could do this through a regular blog, polls, or by having a comment feature added to all articles or stories. These social media tools can really help you learn about and engage with your audience at a deep level. This is one of the emerging aspects of the Web that has accelerated its evolution away from print.

With so many tools available, many site owners throw content against the wall and hope it sticks to some of the folks who come to their site. With modern tools such as polls and blog comments, that can work, as long as you commit to adjusting content to your audience's needs as you go. But we hope you aspire to learn more about your audience before they come to your site. If it works to gain more information about your audience through their comments on your site, why not try to learn more about them through their comments, tags, social bookmarks, and other activities on other sites that include social media functions? This section discusses tactics for mining social media sites to learn more about your target audience, so that you can create more relevant content for them when they get to your site. If you also include social media functions on your site, you can do a better job of adjusting your content to these users.

In speaking about social media below, you will continually see terms such as **tags, tagging, notes,** and **bookmarks.** When they visit sites, people use tags or bookmarks so they can easily return to a given page. These can give you some insight into what words are most popular and into how users build queries. This builds on your knowledge of the keywords that people use when they search. Further, in some cases, these social media tools can show the semantic relationships between words. The keywords that you can glean by exploring social media tools and sites can give you valuable insights into how users perceive your products, services, and content. These will allow you to further understand trends and collect competitive data.

Many sites that feature social tagging to help people find items posted by like-minded users use the **tag cloud** interface (see Figure 5.7). We recommend that you enable social tagging on your site, to find out how people tag your content. We also recommend that you look at competitive sites' implementations of social tagging and see how their users tag content. When you develop keyword clouds as part of the set of seed words in your keyword research, you can compare those to tag clouds to find similar relationships. The basic idea is that tag clouds and keyword clouds are very similar. They both include sets of related words used by Web site visitors to find and catalog content for easier retrieval. If users tag content with some words, they are likely to use the same words in

Figure 5.7   A typical tag cloud interface. Content producers tag pieces of content (in this case RSS feeds) and the application displays the content most often tagged with the same words. Users can slide the bar at the top to display more or fewer tags in the cloud and click and add tags of interest into their personal RSS feed folders. (*Source:* www.ibm.com)

their keyword searches. For example, in the sidebar on tools, the tag cloud generated by Quintura can be used as part of your keyword research to generate a keyword cloud.

Examples of social tagging or social bookmarking sites include digg.com, delicious .com, and flickr.com. IBM is experimenting with using social tagging to help users find content (see Figure 5.7). We plan to mine this tagging data for our keyword research. In addition to tag clouds, we recommend checking out sites with stable social tagging functions, especially www.delicious.com/tag/, a social bookmarking site that lets you see if your keywords are being used as tags and lets you view other complementary tags. Another nifty function at www.delicious.com/url/, lets you see if your URL is being tagged.

Mining Social Media for Keyword Research

You can research how social media authors (such as bloggers) are tagging their content as it relates to your topics or keywords. This can show their popularity, as well as what topical interests are related to your keywords. It's a good idea to get more information about other tags associated with your seed list by using tools such as Omigli, Boardreader, Twing, Ice Rocket (for trending), Technorati, delicious, ReddIt, Digg, Magnolia, StumbleUpon, Filtrbox, Clusty, and the Google AdWords Keyword Tool. Each tool has its own way of showing which keyword tags are the most popular. In some cases, the most insightful information is shown at the bottom of the search results screen. For example, at www.stumbleupon.com, you can search by criteria such as keyword, product, theme, and topic, and then review the "Filter by tag" list. The results are easier to see at http://gnolia.com/tags, which shows a list of tags underneath the results. Many other tools are also available.

Using an economical social media analysis tool such as Alterian SM2, you can export data about social media posts to Excel and then use any text analyzer tool, such as textSTAT, to see the relationships between words, and keywords that are associated with a keyword phrase that you enter (Figure 5.8). This will help you craft your long-tail keywords. Think of SM2 as a social media warehouse. How can we know if we're getting enough of the conversation related to one of our keyword phrases? SM2 has created a distributed database that retrieves 10 billion pieces of data per day (a number that is constantly growing) from user-generated content. It also features an analytical tool that collects information from social media marketing sites, such as Twitter, Blogger, epinion, and Facebook (at the time this was written). SM2 intends to add new networks as they become popular, such as StumbleUpon and Google's Knol.

continues

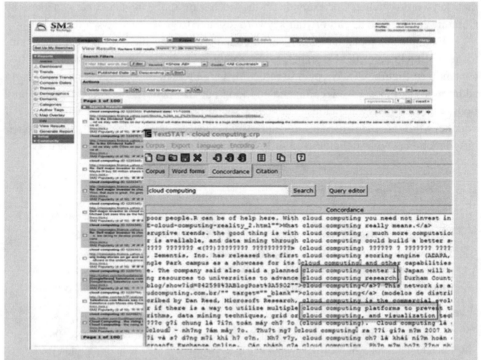

Figure 5.8   This example shows a series of posts around "cloud computing" using the Alterian SM2 tool. You can then export the post contents into TextSTAT to highlight possible new keyword combinations. (Copyright, Alterian 2009)

As you can see from the sidebar, social media analysis tools like Alterian SM2 can help you see how people construct their queries. This can give you insight into word patterns, which ultimately helps you create your long-tail keyword patterns. You can also conduct local SEO through keyword analysis by using tools such as Clusty, a social media search engine (Figure 5.9). For a given keyword phrase that you enter, Clusty queries several top search engines, combines the results, and generates an ordered list of those keywords, based on comparative ranking. This "metasearch" approach helps raise the best results to the top and push search engine spam to the bottom.

In Clusty, you will find categorization or "clusters" (or topics) in the left navigation bar. These may help you see keyword possibilities that you might not have considered otherwise. Clusty also has a "remix" feature that allows you to see one level deeper for other submerged related topics. Using these words in your content will greatly help you increase the relevance of your site.

Figure 5.9 Clusters help you see your search results by topic so you can zero in on exactly what you're looking for or discover unexpected relationships between items. (*Source:* www.clusty.com)

Summary

- Basic SEO only explains a small part of the opportunities that you as a Web content publisher have to provide relevant content to your audience.

- Beyond mere keywords, page purpose is a key element. Users who find your topics relevant one day might not the next if they come to your site with a different purpose in mind. Awareness and consideration are two common purposes in marketing contexts.

- Beyond purpose, you must take several linguistic variables into account to better connect with your audience. Use can use word patterns located from search engines and tools as alternate primary keywords, secondary keywords, or as the core of long-tail keywords.

- Using long-tail keywords can lead to better engagement by attracting people who are deeply interested in your topics. Multi-phrase search queries generally target more interested, potential customers.

- Because there is less competition for multi-phrase search queries, use them to help your long-tail keywords rank better.

- Use social media functions to learn more about the users who find your content through search.

- As important as it is to connect with users who come to your site, it's even more important to use social media functions such as social tagging and bookmarking to validate keyword research with tag cloud research.

- Use keywords located in social media posts to gain insight into search query constructions and patterns. By using social media tools, you can see how your audience is using your keyword terms. You can also see how others are searching, what other words are being used in conjunction with your keywords, and other word possibilities.

- To optimize your pages for search, use words that your target audience or competitors use.

CHAPTER 6

Developing a Search-Optimized Site Architecture

So far we've focused on how to fill Web pages with relevant content for your target audiences. Of course, your pages don't exist in isolation. Preferably, you develop a Web site full of pages as one orchestrated user experience. Your users expect a site with high-level information on the top-level landing pages. And these landing pages lead users to more detailed content, depending on their needs. In this way, your Web experiences are flexible and interactive, giving users the ability to choose exactly the information that is relevant to them.

As noted earlier, this is another way in which Web publishing differs from print publishing. In print, you develop the flow of information and the reader must adapt. Sure, readers can skim and skip sections. But a print publication is designed for linear, serial information processing. The information in one section or chapter builds on previous sections or chapters (as in this book). Print publications have their place. The writer presumes that the reader does not know the information with enough depth to predetermine the optimal information flow. Print readers give up control of information flow and read serially, sometimes consuming marginally relevant content in order to grasp the fullness of a topic.

But on the Web, users are in control. According to Jakob Nielsen (May 2008), readers who scan take an average of 3 to 6 seconds to determine whether a page of content is relevant to them. If it is, they spend an average of 26 seconds consuming the information on that page. Clearly, they have a low tolerance for consuming marginally relevant content. Our goal is to give them easy options to traverse our information in non-linear, interactive ways. This can be a challenge, especially when you consider that an increasing percentage of your visitors arrive in the middle of your site's experience from search engines. It's easy enough to design experiences if you presume that users come to your other pages from your home page—the front door of your site. But how do you account for users who enter through the side door (from Google or other search engines)? Though you can't anticipate your users' every move, you can at least provide cues to help users navigate both to higher-level (more basic or foundational) information and to lower-level (deeper, more detailed) content.

Besides helping visitors find relevant content, having a clear site architecture tends to improve search results, for two reasons. First, internal links improve a page's PageRank—the part of Google's algorithm that ranks pages higher if they are linked to other relevant pages on the Web (see Chapter 7). Though not as important as external links, Google will give you credit for links into your pages from highly relevant pages within your site. Second, the Google crawler mimics human Web navigation, following links in its path through your content. If you design a clear site architecture, you make it easier on the crawler and help ensure that the crawler will find your content and pass its information to the search engine.

Many site owners assume that having a clear site architecture is enough. But developing site architecture for visitors coming from search engines goes a step further. Your primary goal is to help users find the content they need with the fewest number of clicks. Clear site architecture helps them get to relevant content even if they land on a page that is not exactly what they want. And search-optimized site architecture helps them land directly on the most relevant pages in your site. That is the ideal situation for the user, requiring the fewest number of clicks to get to their destination. Search-optimized site architecture starts with keyword clouds and organizes pages around the keywords most relevant to the target audience for each page. In this way, keyword research can tell you not only how to create pages, but whole-site experiences with no gaps or overlaps in the content organized by the clouds of keywords that are most relevant to your target audience.

For a variety of reasons, having a search-optimized site architecture enables your target audience to find relevant content with a minimum of clicks. Web writers, editors, and content strategists need to understand the principles and best practices of effective search-optimized site architecture if they hope to consistently connect with their target audiences.

Developing Clear Information Architecture

Information Architecture (IA) is a discipline in which practitioners analyze intended information tasks and design experiences to make those tasks easier. The discipline touches all areas of information management, including but not limited to library science, software application development, technical communication, and Web development. Each field practices information architecture slightly differently. In Web development, the focus of information architecture efforts is Web usability, of which Nielsen (1999, 2001, 2006, 2008) is a leading practitioner.

Web usability is often divided between two primary fields: design—how a site looks to the user—and navigation design—how the visual elements that users interact with on the screen moves them through a site experience. Visual design gives users the cues they need to understand how to move around in a site. In particular, if users know where to find navigation items on every page, they will at least know where to look for relevant content from any page in your site.

Visual design is important, but for the purposes of a search-optimized site architecture, navigation design is what distinguishes a good Web user experience from a poor one. A site might have a clear page layout, with easy links and icons that give users an idea of what they can expect when they click on them. But if the links don't move them to the content they need, they will eventually abandon the site. Also, search crawlers focus on metadata and text, ignoring visual design. How easy it is for crawlers to find your content determines whether they can index all your content. Even the best visual design can't make up for dead ends, circular paths, or other navigation mistakes.

Navigation design typically begins with **task analysis**, in which designers try to think of all the ways the target audience might need to use the site's information. Task analysis leads to **flow diagrams** and **wireframes,** visual representations of a site based on flow diagrams, which spell out how to make these usage patterns as simple as possible. Task analysis is related to page purpose (covered in Chapter 5)—in the sense that every page on your site must have a defined purpose that supports a node in your site's wireframe. Every node has a defined task, which is defined by the page purpose.

In Chapter 5, we discussed common marketing page purposes, such as awareness, consideration, and interest. When designing a site for audiences interested in a certain product, it is important to serve them the information on that product at the appropriate place in the sales cycle. This is an example of how the scenarios you develop must consider how users move from one page purpose to another, as their tasks demand. Figure 6.1 shows a typical flow diagram of a simplified marketing site experience. Figure 6.2 translates the flow diagram into a wireframe document.

If you combine the visual design with navigation design, you get what we call a site's *architecture*. This consists of domains, main categories pages, and subcategories pages. These pages are also related to the media assets for which they serve as a conduit, such as videos, podcasts, PDFs, presentations, documents, and audio files.

The above process works for cases in which you are trying to re-architect an existing experience, as we describe in the Smarter Planet case study (see sidebar). In the case of Smarter Planet, we were fortunate that the content did not need a major overhaul. We just assigned new keywords to the existing content and the experience was ready to go for the new content as we added it—about half way through the content plan. But what do you do when you need to develop a site architecture from the ground up? In that case, do you start with a content plan, and try to see how the pages within the plan interrelate before developing the flow diagrams and wireframes? Or do you start with the flow diagrams and wireframes and develop a content plan to fill the pages with compelling content?

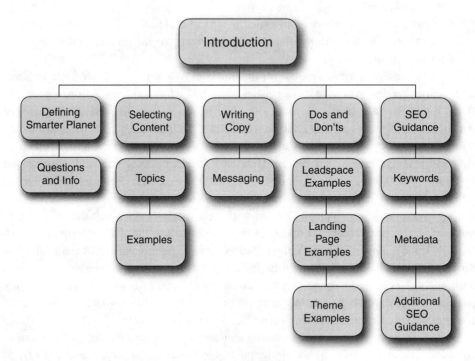

Figure 6.1   Flow chart of Smarter Planet Standards sites with different user tasks.

In our experience, it is usually better to start with the content plan and develop your architecture from it. As the old adage says: Form follows function. Start with a content plan, including items such as your audience, topic, page purposes, and calls to action. Then develop your site architecture to suit the content plan. But when you have the site architecture done, you will need to fit your content to the page templates according to the design, and it might not all fit just right. So you go back and tweak the architecture to allow your content to grow to suit the needs of the audience. And perhaps along the way, you discover gaps or potential overlaps that you did not consider when you developed the content plan.

It is not uncommon to go through several drafts of the site architecture and content plan before publishing. Even then, when you start measuring the results of your new Web site, you will find room for improvement, and places where adjustments are needed. Visitor data will tell you a lot about the effectiveness of your site's experience for your audience. Perhaps user feedback will cue you about an unforeseen gap. Or there may be an apparent conflict between two similar pages. Like most things in Web publishing, developing a clear

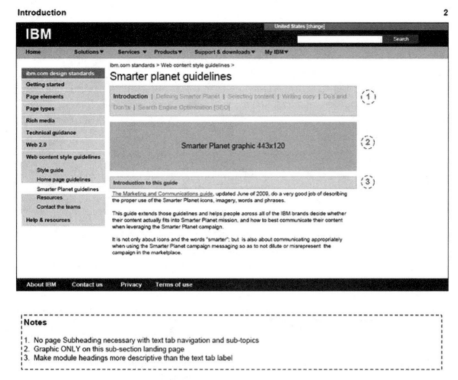

Figure 6.2 Wireframes from the flow diagram.

site architecture based on a content plan is an iterative process. And as in most other areas of Web publishing, you can come closer to your target and reduce revisions if you develop your content plan and site architecture with search engines in mind.

Case Study: Smarter Planet Site Redesign

In late 2008 and the first half of 2009, IBM created a series of Web articles that comprised the Smarter Planet Web experience. The series attempted to define the major problems facing the planet today and to highlight interesting solutions to these problems. For example, Smart Grid technology can solve the problem of electricity waste in power grids. The thought was to promote more instrumented, interconnected, and intelligent solutions to the huge problems facing the planet, such as climate change, world hunger, and world health crises.

continues

As often happens with content efforts of this type, the experience around the Smarter Planet stories grew organically around a centralized Flash experience. This was not bad in the beginning, when there were relatively few Smarter Planet stories in the experience and the goal of the experience was to support an advertising campaign. But the experience became really tough to use as the site grew and the goal for the site evolved into becoming the Web destination for Smarter Planet content. Eventually, IBM needed to redesign the site with a whole new information architecture and a fresh visual design.

One problem with the initial design was that the Flash experience at the home page level of the site got progressively slower and more difficult to use as more content was added. This also caused serious linking issues, because crawlers can't see Flash content. This had two bad consequences. First, Google couldn't index the site's home page. Second, Google's crawler could not follow links in Flash. From the crawler's perspective, each page within the site stood on its own, rather than as spokes of one hub—the home page. This was made worse because there was only one way to get from one page in the experience to another—through the home page.

The goal of the redesign was to develop a clean and elegant user experience that enabled users (and the crawler) to navigate easily from any page to any other page in the experience. In addition, we wanted the design to give users visual cues as to the relevance of the content on the pages, and to make it especially satisfying to people who scanned it. Finally, the site was re-architected from a keyword perspective. Each page was assigned a relevant, high-demand keyword. The keywords were not all from the same cloud, but they had a family resemblance related to the central theme of instrumented, interconnected, and intelligent systems that solve planet-wide problems.

A couple of things to note about the experience highlighted in Figure 6.3 and Figure 6.4: First, the centralized navigation elements are repeated at the top and bottom of each page. The primary benefit to this is that it gives users the ability to navigate anywhere in the experience, whether they are just entering the page or they have read to the bottom of the page. Because the page shown here scrolls for three screens, this was especially important. A secondary benefit is for the crawler. Mouse-over navigation is a cool effect for user experience design. But because crawlers cannot follow links within JavaScript, a primary criterion of the redesign was to provide a non-JavaScript alternative. That appears at the bottom of the page, where the navigation elements from the top are repeated, this time in a format that allowed the crawler to follow the links.

Second, the design allows for a variety of content experiences to live side by side, including magazine-style articles, quick facts and figures, podcasts, links to deeper thought-leadership pieces and case studies, and a user poll. This satisfies the diverse audience that typically consumes content with such a broad appeal. (The broader the appeal of content, the more diverse the audience, as a general rule of thumb.) There is plenty of copy on the page to satisfy hungry spiders, and plenty of quick hitters to satisfy scanners.

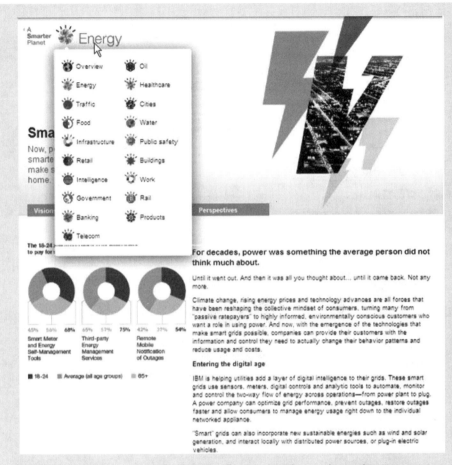

Figure 6.3 The top third of a Smarter Planet experience shows the mouse-over JavaScript navigation to every other page in the experience. Google's crawler cannot follow links in JavaScript, so the experience needed an alternative navigation scheme elsewhere on the page.

The result of the redesign was stunning. Visits to the entire Smarter Planet experience doubled almost as soon as the new design went live. Click-through rates to topics, and engagement as a whole, doubled overnight. Topics that were getting no traffic prior to the redesign suddenly got very good traffic and engagement. In particular, the navigation icons at the bottom of the pages did their job, capturing clicks from topic to topic. The combination of a site re-architecture, a new visual design, and a content refresh using high-demand keywords from the same family turned the site into an IBM best practice.

continues

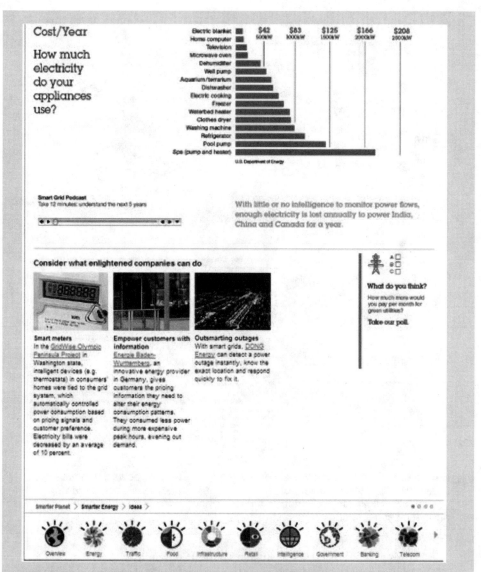

Figure 6.4   The bottom third of the Smarter Planet experience displays the same navigation elements found at the top of the page. But here they are coded in a format other than JavaScript, which can be followed by the crawler.

Developing Search-Optimized Information Architecture

Developing clear site architecture is part of the basic blocking and tackling of Web development. If you're familiar with Web publishing, nothing that we have presented so far should surprise you. But we think clear site architecture is not enough. It's all well and good to have clear paths to the content on your site. This enables visitors to find relevant content even if they came from Google and landed on a page that was not directly relevant to what they were trying to find. But it's even better if you can design your site architecture to make it more likely that they will land directly on pages containing the content they're looking for. This is what we mean by **search-optimized site architecture**.

Just like ordinary clear site architecture, search-optimized site architecture starts with a content plan. But a search-optimized content plan starts with keyword research. From a keyword cloud that is highly relevant to your topic and target audience, you can develop a content plan that covers the cloud completely, without overlap.

Think of a Web site as being like a grocery store. It's ideal if you carry everything your customers want, and nothing more. They don't have to go to other stores to find what they're looking for. And you don't get left with inventory they won't buy. In grocery stores, organizing the aisles into logical product families (and facing the products for easy visual retrieval) will ensure that the customers can quickly find what they need. If they don't, they will leave in frustration to look in another store for the products you carry.

In Web development, content modules are like the products in a grocery store. And pages are like the aisles, in which you organize and face similar content modules, by category, to users. You want to try to develop exactly the content your target audience needs. If you have too much "content inventory" on your shelves, it can actually make it harder for your audience to find what it needs on a topic (not to mention the cost of developing the excess content). If your shelves are bare or lack key content your visitors need, they will go to a competitor to find it. And if your content is not organized in a logical way, they might leave your site in frustration before they find the content you have so painstakingly developed.

We suggest that the most logical, semantic way to organize your content is by keyword relationships. Keyword relationships can help you understand to what extent pages of content are relevant to each other.[1]

Given enough time and attention, visitors could find any piece of content relevant to any other. But their time and attention span are short. To feel that two pieces of content are sufficiently relevant to each other to be worth their time and attention, visitors must see this

---

1. To be clear, content is only relevant to visitors, not to other content. But we say that content is relevant to other content as a short cut for saying that a visitor finds both pieces of content relevant and judges that they are related. For example, two pieces of content on the same product are relevant to each other because visitors can grasp the product-level relationship between them.

quickly. But how can you predict how well visitors will correlate different pages of content on the same site? The easiest and best way is to look at how they use keywords and see what relationships they grasp between pages with keywords in the same cloud or family.

Not coincidentally, starting your content plan with keyword research is also the most effective way to attract a highly targeted audience from search engines. Your site visitors are individuals, with different cultural backgrounds, ethnicities, religions, experiences, geographical origins, and family origins. Two visitors will not use the exact same keywords to describe what they are looking for in Google, even if they are looking for the same thing. And two visitors who are looking for entirely different things might use the same keywords. You will never engage perfectly with your diverse Web audience. But if you cover the range of possibilities as completely as you can, you will do a better job of targeting the diverse set of individuals who share an interest in your content.

Another consideration in any content plan is the linking plan. Links are not merely flat pathways from one page to another. Links themselves convey relevance. A key aspect of gaining link equity (or link juice) from internal links is to have clickable text displayed to users that takes them on the next leg of their journey through your site. If the text of a link to a page matches the keywords on the target page, Google will give you the maximum value for that link. So if you design your pages with keywords in mind, you can write your link text to match the keywords of your destination pages.

For these reasons, it's best to start your content plan with a description of your target audience. Then, perform keyword research into what words and phrases your target audience uses to find similar content. When you do this, you will start to see semantic relationships between the high-demand keywords in the same cloud, so that within your site architecture, you can connect pages based on those keywords. It can also make you more aware of how your target audience uses keywords to find related relevant content.

You can also start to see how to fill gaps in your content plan. As a first pass, you could add high-demand keywords. A second pass might include the keywords in the same clouds as the high-demand keywords. The third pass might include long-tail keywords. You need not get to this level of granularity initially, but the process of developing a content plan from a set of high-demand keywords can go all the way down to the long-tail. The important thing is that keywords can guide you at just about every level of site architecture.

Besides developing the most logical site architecture you can, developing search-optimized site architectures has four main benefits:

1. It enables you to cover the range of possible keyword combinations that your target audience uses, thus capturing a higher proportion of targeted visitors.

2. It enables you to fill gaps in content that you did not appreciate prior to doing keyword research.

3. It enables you to gain market intelligence on your target audience, which helps you better address the needs of the audience that you attract from Google.

4. It enhances internal link equity. Search engines use the same algorithm to assess whether two pages are relevant to each other as they do to judge if a page is relevant to a keyword phrase. If the pages that link to one another on your experience have related keywords, Google will judge them as relevant to each other, and that will tend to increase their PageRank from your internal links.

When you build sites based on your target audience's keyword usage, you ensure that visitors will find the items they need from your grocery store of content. Your pages, or shelves, will be well stocked with all the items that your diverse, but focused, audience needs. And you can minimize empty shelves and reduce redundant page inventory in the process.

Creating Google Site Maps

When you are done with your wireframes and ready to create content with the keywords you have identified (and noted in the header of every page in your wireframe), you need not discard your wireframe document. We recommend reworking it to serve your users as a site map. Site maps are not only a time-tested way for users to easily navigate sites; they're especially easy on the crawler. A crawler that sees the site map and can then follow all the links from it (conveniently organized by keyword) to the individual pages within your experience will tend to have an easier time passing the information on your whole site back to Google.

Links *within* a site map count as internal links for Google's scoring algorithm. If the link names on your pages are closely associated with the keywords in the cloud that you used to develop your content plan, Google will consider those links highly relevant to each other. This will enhance your PageRank as a result.

Google offers a set of Webmaster tools, including Google Sitemap (https://www.google.com/webmasters/tools/docs/en/protocol.html), which enables you to develop site maps from your content. These tools are offered at no cost as of this printing. Google does this because its leadership team knows that its performance depends on its crawler finding the most relevant content for its users. The Google Sitemap tool creates an XML file (based on the Sitemap protocol maintained by the independent standards group sitemap.org) for the express purpose of notifying Google's crawler that you have Web pages available for crawling.

Even if you do not use the Google Sitemap tool, you can create XML-based sitemaps that are in compliance with the sitemap.org standards and with many other tools. Because the structure of a site map should mirror your wireframes, you should always create one for your sites. As soon as your pages go live, you should publish a site map of your content. Then, every page that you add should have a new site map entry associated with it.

continues

> **Note:** Site maps serve two purposes. First, you can publish them on your site to help users navigate—a practice we highly recommend. Second, you can publish them to Google and other search engines to help them crawl your site—a practice we consider essential. In some cases, you can create XML sitemaps that can serve both purposes. But the processes are typically separate and are usually performed by different individuals in a large organization.

Developing a Search-Optimized Information Governance System

So far we've helped you optimize a whole architecture of your own pages. But what if your pages are related to others on your site and you don't own those other pages? How do you collaborate effectively with others in your company who also publish Web content on your site, so that the whole site experience is search optimized?

Perhaps you write for marketing pages and you need to understand content from other parts of the sales cycle, such as support, in order to draw the right audience to your pages. Or perhaps you write for the support organization and you need to collaborate with others in your own organization to ensure that you are all creating an orchestrated content experience for customers who need support. Whatever your role, chances are you have experienced customers coming to your pages from other parts of the site and having trouble with the user experience because that other part of the site does things differently.

One of the main complaints we get at IBM through the "Rate This Page" and "Web Listening Post" Web surveys is that content seems duplicated. If you work on a site with any complexity at all, especially if multiple owners maintain different areas of the site, you will know that it's extremely difficult to keep duplicate content out of the experience. Unless these various owners from different parts of the site have a collaborative governance system, they end up building parallel experiences and competing with one another for the same audiences. In many cases, they even use the same keywords for their pages, which dilutes the effectiveness of any one page on the same topic.

Your organization doesn't have to have the size and scope of IBM to experience the difficulties in sharing content—or even information about content—between content owners who share one site. Even a site with five owners (such as a blog by one of this book's authors, Twinkietown.com) can run into conflicts. The author has written several blog posts, only to be pushed off the front page by collaborators who were unaware of concurrent development. Unless you are the only one responsible for content on your site, chances are that you need a management system that all content owners can access.

Modern content management systems contain content calendar functions, and other features that help Web publishers from different organizations within one company develop content in an orchestrated way. If that describes your current environment, feel free to skip the rest of this section. But if, like IBM, you have multiple content management systems and authoring environments within a large company environment, read on. We have learned some lessons in one of the largest and most complex content management environments in the world. You can put these lessons to use to make your whole Web experience better.

No matter what system you use to govern gaps and overlaps across an enterprise of content with multiple owners, we recommend that you base your underlying structure on keywords. Just as you build a search-optimized site architecture from a set of keyword clouds, so you should base your whole content enterprise on a bank of keyword clouds (see Figure 6.5). Imagine a spreadsheet with the keywords, associated pages, page owners, target audiences, page purposes, related assets, metadata, and other relevant information as the main columns, and individual pages as the rows.

If every content owner from a business has such a spreadsheet of current and planned content, everyone can plan and execute content that does not overlap with existing or reserved keywords. Without that information, content owners might create their content as a multitude of unrelated, unconnected sites under one domain. This leads to poor search optimization, and to a failure to connect your target audience with relevant content. So a centralized management system is a must for large enterprise content teams. It all starts

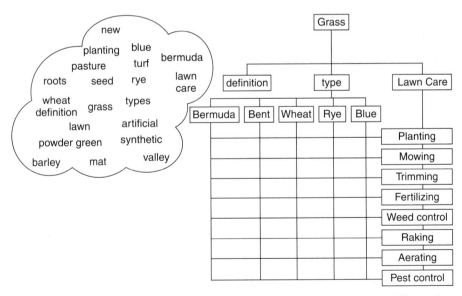

Figure 6.5 Using Quintura, we developed a keyword cloud around the word "Grass." From that, we made a site map.

with keyword clouds and then proceeds with a content, site architecture and linking strategy. Publishing the content is just the first step. As the multiple related pages on a site evolve, they need a common metrics platform by which to judge how the orchestrated experience is performing as a whole. See Chapter 9 for information on that topic.

Summary

- Pages are not developed in isolation, but in the context of an entire site experience.
- Unlike print information experiences, Web experiences must be flexible and interactive, allowing users to create the experience that best suits their needs.
- Gearing Web pages for your users starts with a clear site architecture, which makes it easy to follow the paths through a site to get to their destination.
- Clear site architecture helps users and search crawlers find what they're looking for. It also helps improve the PageRank for your pages.
- Clear site architecture is not enough, however. You also need to develop search-optimized site architecture.
- Search-optimized site architecture starts with keyword research to develop a content plan that matches the high-demand search terms that your target audience uses to describe topics related to yours. If necessary, the plan can proceed to the keyword clouds around the high-demand keywords, and, ultimately, to the long-tails. The content plan spawns a flow diagram and, ultimately, wireframes that detail the site experience for the user.
- Developing pages from these wireframes is an iterative process, often resulting in many drafts and revisions.
- After a set of pages is published, tuning the experience for the target audience is also an iterative process involving page effectiveness metrics, page and link changes, republishing, and additional metrics.
- In larger organizations, content owners must work together through a collaborative management system to reduce keyword competition, content overlaps, and confusing interlinking.

CHAPTER 7

Gaining Credibility through PageRank

Keywords mean different things in different contexts. For example, the word *track* is either a noun or a verb. The noun form refers to the sport involving foot races, the place where various races are held, an essential part of vehicles such as tanks, or a part of a rail line on which trains run. The verb form refers to the act of following game in hunting or checking on the progress of a project. And these are only a few of the uses of the word *track*. Not all words in the English language have multiple dictionary definitions, but those that don't carry varied nuances, depending on the context. And puns, sarcasm, irony, and other forms of linguistic complexity are commonplace in natural language. The Web, of course, contains all of them.

In oral contexts, it is usually easy for us to determine what a person means when she uses a word with varying meanings. By paying attention to a string of words, utterances, and gestures from a speaker, we can usually determine the meaning of *track,* based on those contextual cues. In print contexts, we have all kinds of contextual cues at the macro level, including the cover of the publication, the table of contents, who the author is, and what magazine we're reading. At the micro level, the part of speech is determined by the grammar of a sentence, and the surrounding sentences help determine, for example, whether *track* refers to the sport or the venue.

Because we learned language naturally, we can tune into these contextual cues to determine the usage of a word that has multiple meanings. It's one of the marvels of humanity that we manage to communicate, tell jokes, write lyrics, and use language in innovative ways on a daily basis. But computers don't have humans' ability to pick up on contextual cues surrounding word forms. They rely on raw data—strings of letters, spaces, and punctuation marks—to parse the semantics of human language. Practitioners of Artificial Intelligence (AI) have tried for decades to get computers to mimic human language use, with limited success. The closest they have come is to attach all kinds of structure to the language and related code to help computers determine the context and parse the semantics. This structure is in the form of automated metadata.

On the Web, which is a giant repository of unstructured text, AI-like functions are still a work in progress.[1] In the absence of sufficiently capable AI functions, search engines must somehow make sense of this mass of unstructured human text. At one time in the Web's evolution, search engines relied exclusively on the semantics of the text on a Web page to determine the relevance of the page to a search query. But because of the complexity of the English language, this didn't work too well.

Readers who used search in the mid-90s can attest to what an ineffective experience search was without any contextual cues to rely on. If you searched on the word *track*, you were likely to get pages with *track* in every part of speech, and every conceivable meaning. Sorting through this mess was easier than blind surfing, but not much. Standards groups such as the W3C tried to improve the retrievability of Web pages by adding metadata and other structure to HTML, and later, to XML. But many of these standards were quickly exploited by rogue page owners, to the point where the search experience for users didn't improve much. In the case of metadata, for example, many page owners added irrelevant metadata just to pump up their traffic numbers.

The advent of Google was game changing, for two reasons. First, it required content transparency. It banned results from pages that used metadata spamming and other tricks to get better search visibility. In part because of metadata spamming, Google does not use metadata as part of its relevance algorithm. (However, it does use some metadata to build its search engine results page [SERP]). For example, it uses a page's metadescription in the snippet it displays on its SERP—but not for ranking.) Second, and most importantly, Google engineers and architects figured out a way to use the structure of the Web to determine the context of a Web page for a given search query.[2] It's called PageRank, and it is an increasingly important aspect of writing for the Web. It's also the reason that Google can ignore metadata for its SERP rankings and still lead the market in search usability. The basic idea is that links provide context for Web pages. The structure of the Web can be parsed by mapping its links. Google was the first company to do this, and this fact, more than any other, led to its market dominance.

Following Google's lead, other search engines, such as Yahoo and Bing, pay a lot more attention to links than they once did. Like Google's, the Bing and Yahoo algorithms are trade secrets. But we can infer from our tests that links are also very important to other

---

1. Companies such as IBM have quietly been making progress on AI-like functions to enhance aspects of information retrievability. For example, the UIMA framework allows various linguistic applications such as XQuery, LSI, and LanguageWare to combine their power into one pipeline of enhanced linguistic information about unstructured text on the Web. But these are yet to be widely used and are not used by either Google or Bing to enhance their search engines.

2. Jon Kleinberg, a professor at Cornell, was perhaps the first to recognize that the Web is not just a repository of unstructured text. One can infer the Web's structure by carefully mapping links from page to page and topic to topic. Google uses concepts from Kleinberg (1997) as the basis for its PageRank algorithm.

search engines, including Bing and Yahoo. But based on our extensive research, it is clear that neither Bing nor Yahoo pays as much attention to inbound links as Google. Still, optimizing for Google, which is the clear market leader, will not hurt you with Yahoo or Bing. So we focus on optimizing for Google in this book.

The following italicized passage is Google's own definition of how it determines which pages are listed on its (SERP), and in what order:

- *Page Rank Technology: PageRank reflects our view of the importance of Web pages by considering more than 500 million variables and 2 billion terms. Pages that we believe are important pages receive a higher PageRank and are more likely to appear at the top of the search results.*

  PageRank also considers the importance of each page that casts a vote, as votes from some pages are considered to have greater value, thus giving the linked page greater value. We have always taken a pragmatic approach to help improve search quality and create useful products, and our technology uses the collective intelligence of the Web to determine a page's importance.

- *Hypertext-Matching Analysis: Our search engine also analyzes page content. However, instead of simply scanning for page-based text (which can be manipulated by site publishers through meta-tags), our technology analyzes the full content of a page and factors in fonts, subdivisions and the precise location of each word. We also analyze the content of neighboring web (sic) pages to ensure the results returned are the most relevant to a user's query.* Source: www.google.com/corporate/tech.html[3]

What Google calls the "hypertext-matching analysis" aspect of its algorithm is covered in Chapter 4, in which keyword density, position and other factors—called **on-page factors**—determine the page relevance. PageRank then determines both the contextual relevance and the "importance" or credibility of a page.

Because Google doesn't give us a lot of detail about its proprietary algorithm, it's important to understand it from a more objective perspective. Rand Fishkin of SEOmoz.com surveyed the top experts in the field and came up with Figure 7.1 to demonstrate this.

As Figure 7.1 shows, about 15 percent of Google's algorithm uses on-page elements such as the heading and title tag to determine the semantics of the page itself. Link issues (authority and anchor text of external links) are roughly 42 percent of Google's algorithm. (Google doesn't release information about the exact weighting of different elements in PageRank. We can only infer it from the inputs and outputs of Google's SERP.)

---

3. According to Google representatives we spoke with, "PageRank is one of more than 200 signals we use to determine the rank of a Web site."

Overall Ranking Algorithm

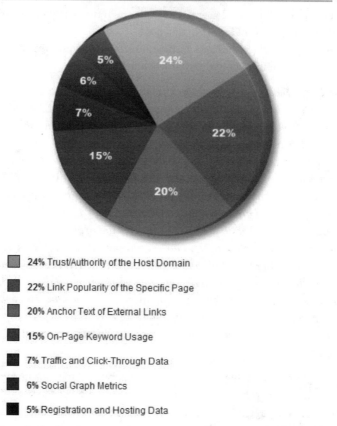

24% Trust/Authority of the Host Domain

22% Link Popularity of the Specific Page

20% Anchor Text of External Links

15% On-Page Keyword Usage

7% Traffic and Click-Through Data

6% Social Graph Metrics

5% Registration and Hosting Data

Figure 7.1   The relative importance of external links to on-page keyword usage in the Google algorithm. Rand Fishkin surveyed 100 top SEO experts about what they thought were the most important reasons that pages rank highly in Google. (*Source:* Rand Fishkin, SEOmoz, Inc, 2009- www.seomoz.org/article/search-ranking-factors)

Of all the aspects of the Web that differentiate it from oral or print media, Hypertext is the most significant. The text on the Web might be unstructured, but the *relationship* between different pieces of text is highly structured. The links between pieces of text are the contextual cues that help determine the natural relevance of one piece of text to another. PageRank uses this feature of the Web to help determine the contextual relevance of a page to a search query, rather than using metadata and other artificial structures in a page's code. Links help Google judge which pages are most contextually relevant to a search query.

If one page links to another and both have related on-page semantics, Google will consider them contextually relevant to each other. The more of these links to and from relevant pages that you have, the easier it is for Google to validate the relevance of your pages for the keywords you identify. In this way, links do a much better job of helping Google determine relevance than metadata does. Because it is much more difficult to create fake links than to fake metadata, links also provide Google with more reliable contextual information about a page.

PageRank doesn't just help Google determine the contextual relevance of a page. It also helps Google evaluate its credibility. A link to a page is often described as a "vote of confidence for that page" (Moran and Hunt, 2005). Google users don't care only about which pages are most linguistically relevant to their search query. They also want the most authoritative information on a topic. On-page semantics can't help a machine determine authority. But links can. The more relevant links there are into a page, the more content owners determine that the page is credible. But Google doesn't treat all links the same. Links from authoritative sites mean more than other links. Simply put, the quantity and quality of links into a page determine its PageRank, which then increases its visibility in Google accordingly. Unpacking how this works, and how to write for PageRank, is the subject of this chapter.

As we see in IBM, it is becoming increasingly difficult to get good visibility in Google with on-page attributes alone. Part of this is competition. Because it's relatively easy to optimize your pages for keywords, more and more content owners are doing it. To compete with them, you must find ways of building links into your pages. Also, Google is not a static application. It has evolved over the years to create a better user experience, based on its own set of metrics. Because it's relatively easy for site owners to manage what's on their pages, Google doesn't count these features as heavily as links. Even if links were as important as on-page elements, PageRank is gaining in importance in the market, as competition for high-demand words increases.

Becoming a Hub of Authority

Having links into your pages is called **link equity** or **link juice**. Suppose that Google assigns points on a scale of 0 to 10 to links, based on the credibility of a site. A highly credible site might warrant 10 points of link juice to the referred page. A lesser site might only garner one point. If two sites have identical page attributes (such as title tags, H1 tags, keywords in the URL, and keyword prominence and density), the one with more link juice will get higher visibility in the search results.

Again, Google does not release its PageRank algorithm, because it is its most important intellectual property. Also, because it's evolving constantly, Google would have to publish changes to the weights and measures of the algorithm on an almost daily basis. But it has used PageRank as at least half its algorithm for so long that we can infer the basic workings of the PageRank portion of the algorithm. Also, how Google determines what pages are the most authoritative on a topic is continually changing with the landscape of the Web. But Google doesn't make this determination itself; it uses the way content owners "vote" for sites they find credible by linking to them. A link to a site is a vote of confidence for it. Links from pages with the most link equity transfer the most link juice. A link from a page without much link equity doesn't carry much link juice.

PageRank is designed to ensure that the most relevant, authoritative sites are listed at the top of search results. The primary way that a site gains authority is by publishing insightful, accurate, or definitive information in a compelling way, so that other sites will link to it. Content that does this is called **link bait.** There is no magic formula for publishing link bait. Good Web content speaks for itself. Link bait comes in many forms— such as white papers, bylined articles, and blogs from popular bloggers. One thing all link bait typically has in common is a byline: People consider the source when they decide to link to a piece of link bait. If two bloggers say the same thing, the one with more credibility in the community— the one with the bigger name—will tend to get the link. If you are just developing credibility in a community, the best way to create link bait is to write something insightful and original—something that no one else has written. If you do that repeatedly over time, eventually your stature in the community will increase and your content will be link bait, even when you are just synthesizing what others have written, in a compelling or interesting way.

Once you create link bait, there are ways of making sure that relevant, authoritative sites find and link to your link bait. The primary way is to find out what the community of people with similar interests is writing and then find your niche within that community. This is one area in which Web publishing resembles certain print contexts. Specifically, in academic publishing, the most effective way to get published is to read the writings of like-minded researchers on your topics of interest. If you find holes or gaps in their research, you design a research proposal to fill one of them. If your research makes a positive contribution to the literature for that topic and theoretical lens, you have a chance to get published in that journal. In this way, link juice is like citations in a print journal. The more citations an article has in the other writers' bibliographies, the more credibility it has. A citation is very similar to a link in the sense that the writer who cites another is giving the other writer a vote of confidence.

To get other people to link to your content, you need to get a vote of confidence from them that your content is worth reading. It costs next to nothing to link to someone's content (whereas publishers have to justify the expense of printing an article in an academic journal). But it is not without risk. Suppose that a content provider publishes a link and a description to your content and her regular visitors find the link irrelevant and have a negative experience with your content. A negative experience with your content is, by association, a negative experience with her content. This is the problem Google faces as it determines what to promote on its search results pages. For this reason, these votes of confidence are not easy to come by. You have to earn them by developing a relationship of trust with the referring site owner. And, of course, you need to create link bait, which is perhaps the biggest challenge.

The main similarity between academic print publishing and getting link equity is that for a particular topic, the Web is a collective effort of like-minded content owners. It takes many authors to fill a quarterly academic journal with good content. In a sense, these folks are collaborating on creating a body of knowledge related to a topic. Except in rare circumstances, content owners can't "own" a whole topic. They need the help of others. And so do you if you wish to publish on the Web. You can't do it by yourself.

If you try to become *the* expert on a topic and set out to publish the definitive reference on it, you will not likely succeed on the Web. Much of the work you publish already exists on the Web. And that information already has link equity in Google. Few people will link to your content if you try to publish the definitive reference in isolation. They will continue to link to the existing information unless your information is clearly superior. But they won't know about your information if you publish it in isolation. They will only find out about it by visiting sites that link to your content, principally Google.

Of course, as we have been writing for several chapters now, Web publishing is different than print publishing in many ways. In one way it is easier to publish on the Web than in an academic journal. Academic journals are typically formal, fixed, rigid communities of insiders. But the Web is an informal community of diverse individuals from all walks of life. So there are fewer barriers to success on the Web. But the Web and academic journals do share one barrier to success: You must join a community of like-minded content producers if you have any hope of success.

In the print world, copyright is a big issue. Freelance writers hire lawyers to examine their contracts and try to ensure that they will ultimately own the rights to their intellectual property. Companies that own intellectual property are very guarded about their proprietary information. Much of it is confidential and is only shared on a need-to-know basis. This works for print because the object is to get the information into the hands of a select few to consume it. Printing information for people who don't understand or appreciate it is a waste of time, labor, ink, and paper.

However, on the Web, it does *not* work to restrict information. If you protect your information behind firewalls accessed only by an exclusive group of individuals with passwords, very few people will find or want it. They will go elsewhere to find similar information, or they will create a free version themselves. Magazines have tried to force users to subscribe to their content on the Web, with little to no success. (One of this book's authors—James Mathewson—was the editor of a magazine —*ComputerUser*—that tried that.) Given the abundance of free information, Web users simply will not tolerate a logon screen and will look elsewhere for similar content. Information wants to be free on the Web, because Web users expect it to be free and will not tolerate needing to pay for it.

On the Web, the value of content is directly proportional to how many links point to it. If you restrict access, you prevent links to your content and degrade its value. Even more of a problem for content owners who try to restrict their content is the fact that crawlers cannot get through firewalls. Content behind a firewall will not appear in Google. And no one will publish a link to a logon screen page. By restricting access to content, you reduce its value to virtually nil.

Case Study: Wikipedia Demonstrates the Value of Free and Open Content on the Web

The Encyclopedia Britannica produced an online version of its reference text and charged people for access. As a result, users who didn't want to pay for information because they thought it should be free and open to the public decided to work together to create their own online encyclopedia, based on a technology called the **wiki**.

Using wiki technology, and a lot of collective sweat and elbow grease, Wikipedia was born, with the goal of being a free, collaborative encyclopedia, to which anyone could contribute. In the beginning, it was woefully inadequate. It had to recruit subject matter experts who were willing to create content for free so that the public could have access to a free encyclopedia. This was a new concept for people who were used to charging by the word. Eventually, the project gained momentum. Now, many people consider it on a par with Encyclopedia Britannica in terms of its authority. The main difference is that relatively few people go to Encyclopedia Britannica online for the information they can get on Wikipedia. Part of the reason is Google: Wikipedia holds the top position in Google for thousands of keywords (for which Britannica is not even in its index). So, when people search on one of those keywords, they often click through to the Wikipedia page for the information.

Wikipedia is in the top position for thousands of keywords in Google precisely because lots of people link to the Wikipedia page for those keywords. Also, it is collaboratively produced by one of the largest and most diverse communities of subject matter experts in the world. As such, Wikipedia is a model of how to publish on the Web. It is a model shared by those who publish work with a Creative Commons license, and for open source software developers. Web content is meant to be freely passed around. The more restrictions you place on it, the less successful you will be in getting the community to accept your work and bless it with link juice.

In terms of link juice, Wikipedia is the ultimate hub of authority. Millions of people link to it. It links to millions of sites. And it is listed as the top result in Google for almost every keyword you can think of. All because a few people got fed up and didn't want to pay for basic information about subjects of interest.

How Wikipedia gained its status should be a lesson to all content owners on how to be a hub of authority. Among other things:

- Start small.

- Don't try to do too much by yourself. Solicit help from colleagues both inside and outside of your company to link to your pages and to build pages to link to— filling holes as much with your own work as with the work of others.

- Be patient and persistent. Test your content as often as possible and adjust as necessary.

- Be transparent about your content, including acknowledging when it needs help (a large number of Wikipedia pages have this warning on them).

- Wherever possible, allow your users to contribute to your content, with reviews, feedback, comments, and the like.

How Not to Get Link Juice

Google is very vigilant about sniffing out scams that attempt to trick its algorithm to artificially improve a page's ranking. In addition to pieces of code that expunge from its index pages suspected of keyword spamming or engaging in link-equity Ponzi schemes, it has hired more than 1,000 editors to audit the search results for high-demand keywords and ensure that the highest-visibility pages are authoritative.

Even if you're not trying to trick Google but are honestly working to get link juice from content owners, you might unwittingly suffer the wrath of Google's protections against link schemes. Because the majority of Google's efforts to thwart dishonest Web site owners are based on code (rather than on content), you can inadvertently trigger the programs that scan for link building schemes.

The first impulse of folks trying to get link juice from similar sites is to simply request a link from them. By that we mean contacting the owners of a site and asking them to link to your content. In our experience, this is not very effective. The typical response contains at least one of the following: "I'll link to your content if you put a link to my content on your home page," or "I'll link to your content if you pay me to do so." If that's the response you get, don't act on it. If the owner doesn't find your content relevant enough to link to it without link-swap or payment conditions, it's not worth pursuing.

Effective sites don't try to do too much, but rely on other sites for supporting information or commentary. In this way, links out of a site have value if they give users a more complete picture of the story the site is trying to tell. A site owner should want to link to you if it improves her users' information experiences. If she demands something more than a better user experience for her visitors, it's an indication that she's not the kind of site owner you want to get links from.

Part of Google's algorithm looks for reciprocal links (links to and from two related sites) and flags a page for elimination if it contains too many of them. Of course, sometimes links can be naturally reciprocal. Two content owners can legitimately admire each others' work and share links. But that is the exception to the norm. If a content owner is not willing to recognize the value of your content for his users, he's likely to own the kind of site that Google has on a watch list for link swapping schemes. Worse yet, you might not be aware of all his content activities. If he demands reciprocity in exchange for an innocent link request, what might he do with others?

A common way to gain link juice, which prompted Google to increase its vigilance towards link swapping is called a **link farm**. This is a group of sites that all link to each other in order to artificially improve their Google visibility. These sites send users round and round in a circle. But they don't really care about users' experience. Because Web advertising is often based on traffic, they just want the visibility they get from Google to increase their ad revenue, without concern for whether they are helping their users understand the content they're looking for. These are the sites Google bans from its index for deceiving their users. If you inadvertently swap links with one of these sites, you might end up on Google's naughty list as well.

Some unscrupulous sites will request links from you. You should be wary of them for the same reasons. Areas of the Web where link farms and other nefarious sites (such as porn and gambling sites) live are called **bad neighborhoods**. Whatever you do, make sure that your links don't end up in a bad neighborhood. Google will penalize you severely for associating with them. They're not always easy to spot, because they can be good at making themselves look like a legitimate site. There are some indicators, however. Link farms and bad neighborhoods commonly are based around the same **Class C IP address**. The Class C part of the address is the third of four sets of numbers in the IP string. If you see that many of the sites trying to develop a link swapping relationship with you have the same Class C address, ignore their requests (see Figure 7.2).

Figure 7.2   The Class C IP address refers to the third of the four sets of numbers in the address.

Because link swapping is mostly ineffective and risky, we don't recommend expending much energy on it. Instead, we recommend focusing on developing your credibility within the community of site owners whose users share the interests of your users, as discussed below.

How to Leverage Existing Relationships to Get Link Juice

In general, we suggest that you develop recognition within the community of site owners related to your topic area. Some of the tactics you can use to develop this credibility are more effective than others. Because the Web is a social medium, in which content areas are built around communities of like-minded sites, taking advantage of the social nature of the Web is the most effective strategy. The two main tactics within this strategy are to

- Take advantage of existing relationships.
- Build new relationships through participation in social media sites such as LinkedIn, Twitter and Facebook. We will cover existing relationships in this section.

The first step in developing a link juice plan is to take an inventory of the people and organizations with whom you have an existing relationship. Chances are, you are not taking advantage of these communities as much as you can. These relationships include colleagues within your company who publish Web pages, colleagues within your company who publish press releases and other media-facing materials, colleagues within partner organizations, and friends and peers from professional or academic associations you belong to (see Figure 7.3).

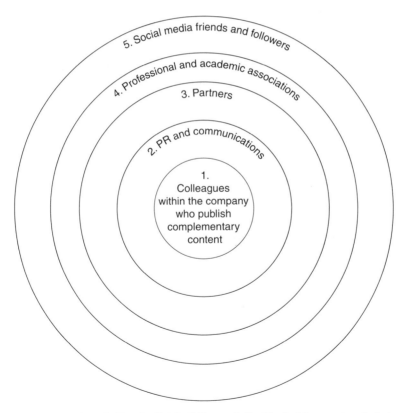

Figure 7.3   The circles of effort for link building activity. Start at the center circle because it contains the easiest avenues of obtaining links, and work your way out.

Start with colleagues in your company who develop content on similar or related topics. Find link opportunities to and from their sites and make link requests to them. Be sure to include instructions about the link text you want your colleagues to use in your request. As a refresher, recall that link text is text that is clickable. Google's crawler looks at link text to determine the relevance of the link to the page it refers to. If the link text contains prominent keywords that also occur in the referred page, the crawler will determine that the link is indeed relevant and will pass that information to Google's algorithms for analysis of how much link juice it warrants.

Links within your site to your own pages do not carry as much link juice as external links coming to your site. But they should be the easiest to get. And if you practice the litmus test that we advocate—asking yourself if the link helps the user's experience—internal links can also help your users find relevant content on your site, which is the point of search engine optimization. So, as part of the basic blocking and tackling of Web publishing, always identify link partners within your company and collaborate to exchange links and descriptions with them, whenever it will improve the user experience for your audience. (We covered this in more detail in Chapter 6.)

If you work for a company, chances are that it publishes press releases announcing product launches and other events of interest to the general public. These are excellent avenues to getting external links. Media outlets often use press releases as the basis of articles about a company. If your press releases are optimized, they will have links to the most relevant pages on your Web site. These links often end up in articles on external sites. There is no better source of external links than this, if you use the right format for your press releases. See Figure 7.4 for an effective press release template.

Case Study: Merging Marketing and Communication to Ensure Better Linking Collaboration

At IBM, every time we release a new product, we publish a lot of materials to help promote it. These include press releases, Web pages, and reams of collateral. The press releases are written for media outlets that we hope will publish articles about the product. The Web pages are created for potential customers to learn about the product and find out how to buy it. The organizations that create these two sets of materials—the communications division for press releases, and the marketing division for Web pages—are traditionally not managed by the same branch of a company. At one time, IBM was no different.

Before the Web took a central role in our marketing efforts, this was not a problem. Because the two sets of materials served different audiences, it was natural that they were created by different departments. But when the Web became the center of our marketing efforts, we realized that we could use press releases as a source of link

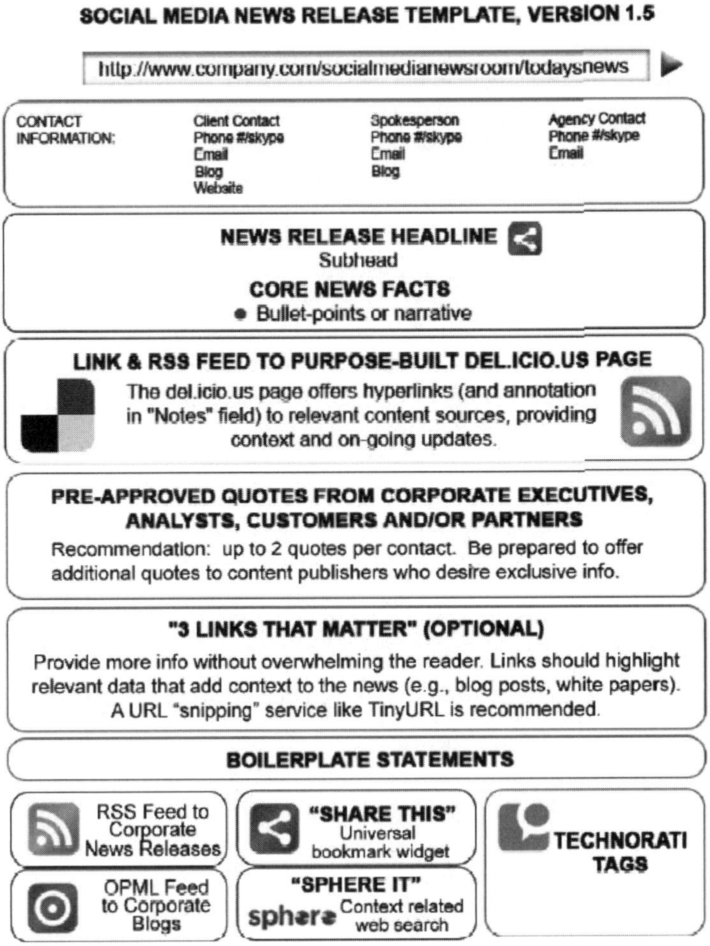

SOCIAL MEDIA NEWS RELEASE TEMPLATE, VERSION 1.5

http://www.company.com/socialmedianewsroom/todaysnews ▶

CONTACT
INFORMATION:

Client Contact
Phone #/skype
Email
Blog
Website

Spokesperson
Phone #/skype
Email
Blog

Agency Contact
Phone #/skype
Email

NEWS RELEASE HEADLINE
Subhead
CORE NEWS FACTS
● Bullet-points or narrative

LINK & RSS FEED TO PURPOSE-BUILT DEL.ICIO.US PAGE
The del.icio.us page offers hyperlinks (and annotation in "Notes" field) to relevant content sources, providing context and on-going updates.

PRE-APPROVED QUOTES FROM CORPORATE EXECUTIVES, ANALYSTS, CUSTOMERS AND/OR PARTNERS
Recommendation: up to 2 quotes per contact. Be prepared to offer additional quotes to content publishers who desire exclusive info.

"3 LINKS THAT MATTER" (OPTIONAL)
Provide more info without overwhelming the reader. Links should highlight relevant data that add context to the news (e.g., blog posts, white papers). A URL "snipping" service like TinyURL is recommended.

BOILERPLATE STATEMENTS

RSS Feed to Corporate News Releases

"SHARE THIS"
Universal bookmark widget

TECHNORATI TAGS

OPML Feed to Corporate Blogs

"SPHERE IT"
sphere Context related web search

Figure 7.4　A press release template that includes links and social media elements. (*Source:* Swif Communications 2009)

juice by publishing links to the marketing sites within the press release. The thought was, if a media outlet decided to publish a story based on the press release, it might also publish the link on its Web site. As highly credible sources, those links would bring a lot of link juice with them. For example, if Ziff Davis published a story about our product and linked to the appropriate product page, that page would get good search visibility. If it didn't link to the page because the press release didn't have the right link, the product page didn't get good search visibility. It was that simple.

continues

> To help improve the coordination between Marketing and Communications, IBM has merged the two groups under one executive. In this role, the executive has developed an internal social media system to encourage collaboration between marketing and communications professionals within the company. We have posted standards and education within the system to ensure that press releases contain the right links. We are also developing follow-up procedures that include information about using the links that we publish in our press releases. When companies like Ziff Davis include a link, it helps their readers, who might want to learn more about the IBM product by visiting the IBM site for the product. So it serves Ziff Davis's readers better to give them an opportunity to click directly to the page for the product. And, of course, it's better for the Web page about the product, because that Ziff Davis link creates link juice and, ultimately, visibility for the product page.

Most companies work with partners to help them do a better job of serving their customers. The more closely you work with your partner, the better that service becomes. But for some reason, that close relationship does not always extend to the Web. Customers who come to a partner site looking for information on how the partner helps them use your product should naturally be interested in linking to information on your product. But few companies help their partners link appropriately. Of course, every link to a partner page from your page provides link juice for the partner page. And vice versa—every link into your site from partner pages brings your pages link juice. Besides internal linking, nothing should be easier than getting partners to link to your pages. And unlike internal links, links from partners can carry a lot of link juice. We recommend identifying partner opportunities and working with partners to build links into their pages (with the appropriate anchor, or link text).

A lot of writers and editors belong to professional groups or alumni organizations. Perhaps you attend conferences related to them. You will meet lots of like-minded people at these gatherings. Chances are, they have a Web site. If the site is closely related to your own, to the point where links between your site and a peer's site would improve users' experience, it is wise to take advantage of these relationships. Beyond conferences, social media sites such as LinkedIn and Facebook can help you keep in touch with your peers. We also recommend promoting new content in your site's status updates and tweets as a way of keeping your peers informed about new content. If they have a related Web site and find your content useful for their audience, they will pick up the links. These kinds of natural links can really help your pages gain link juice, especially if you have a lot of friends who produce authoritative Web sites.

Using Social Media to Develop Linking Relationships

Before social media became popular, professional networking required a lot of hard work. People attended conferences, passing their business cards around. Perhaps they even presented. Another way to gain visibility was to publish. Whether in academic or professional journals, publishing helps people get noticed by peers. Speaking at conferences and publishing in journals were once the primary ways of gaining credibility among the community of experts on topics of expertise. Social media sites have changed all that.

Now experts have blogs and LinkedIn, Facebook, and Twitter accounts, and they get the word out on their latest work by posting or tweeting about it. Rather than needing to gain friends in their fields through hard weeks of travel, they can gain friends and followers daily, without leaving their desks. Not only can they promote their content, they can find good content to link to by following the right people on Twitter and making a select few of the people they follow friends on Facebook. Social media has automated the art of the conference, and it has accelerated the pace of finding potential collaboration partners.

You might be tempted to think that every link you create to your own content on Facebook or Twitter gets you link juice directly. To do this would be tantamount to creating content on Wikipedia in order to gain link juice. But although Wikipedia is the ultimate hub of authority, it will not directly get you any link juice. Why? Link juice is supposed to be a natural phenomenon. The folks at Google do not want to encourage people to publish content on one public site and link to it on another site just to get link juice. This is rigging the system. So they created an HTML attribute value, as part of the W3C 2.0 rel specification. It's called the *nofollow* attribute value—a piece of code (`rel=nofollow`), which can be added to the HTML of a link and prevents it from passing link juice. All the links in Wikipedia are *nofollow* links, so you do not get any link juice if Wikipedia developers link to your page.

Other sites that typically carry the *nofollow* attribute value on links include Facebook, Twitter, YouTube, StumbleUpon, and Delicious. You cannot manufacture link juice for your own site by cleverly using social media sites to develop links into your content. Nonetheless, using social media sites is perhaps the most effective way to get link juice. How? Social media sites are places where you can connect with experts in your field and promote your content, much as you would do at a conference. If friends and followers find that your content helps them better serve their audience, they are likely to publish your link and pass it around to their friends and followers. Each of those links then carries the link juice appropriate to your friends' or followers' sites.

A Handy Tool to Find Nofollow Links

If you use Firefox, you can use the SearchStatus Firefox plug-in to find *nofollow links. After installation, it displays information at the lower right of the browser screen (see Figure 7.5).* The tool is currently offered at no cost and is easily downloaded from the Firefox plug-ins page (https://addons.mozilla.org/en-US/firefox/search?q=SearchStatus&cat=all). With the **Highlight Nofollow links** option checked, every site you visit will display with the *nofollow* links highlighted. Visit Wikipedia, and you will see that all links are highlighted in pink.

Figure 7.5   Firefox Search Status tool options menu.

In addition to being promotional vehicles, the main value of social media sites for your content is to help you find and connect with as many experts in your field as you can. One of the greatest difficulties in becoming a hub of authority is getting to know all the experts in your field. Suppose you are working on an important piece of content, but another expert in your field has proven that your research is a nonstarter. Unless you know about your colleague's work, you might go ahead and do a lot of fruitless research. Developing a large and focused set of friends and followers can help you overcome this challenge.

Writing for social media sites is an emerging art form that deserves a chapter all its own (Chapter 8). But for the present, suffice it to say writing for social media is much less formal and much more conversational and pithy than writing for other Web pages. Like all writing, writing for social media is about writing for your audience. The difference is that you often know your audience very well in social media settings, so you can tailor it to their particular modes of expression. This might include puns, irony, or emotionally laden posts. On ordinary Web pages, you must respect the diversity of your audience by writing in compelling ways that leave little room for creative interpretation. Unless you have a vast set of friends and followers who are as diverse as an ordinary Web audience, social media sites allow you more freedom of expression.

Writing for social media also bears similarities to writing for ordinary Web pages. The primary similarity is that the most effective posts and tweets contain links to work you want to highlight—your own, and work from friends and followers.

The one constant on the Web is that the value of content is directly proportional to the quality and quantity of links into it. That is true on Twitter, Wikipedia, and, of course, Google.

Using the Power of the Web to Get Link Juice

In social media sites, you'll notice that compared to other sites, they have a higher density of rich media content and a lower density of text. People use the social media sites to share videos via YouTube, presentations via SlideShare, photos via Flickr, and podcasts via iTunes. These rich media file sharing sites have innovative user interfaces that feature user reviews, social tagging—interfaces that allow users to attach tags in the form of words to pieces of content as a means of finding and sharing relevant content—and social bookmarking—interfaces that enable users to create and share bookmarks to favorite content. They become treasure troves of content that social media mavens use to spice up their posts and tweets.

Though this book is primarily about writing for the Web, we would be remiss if we did not mention that your content strategy needs to include using these social file sharing sites to connect with your audience, especially as a means of building links into your content. The best Web pages feature a mix of media: presentations, PDFs, videos, and podcasts. The emerging trend in Web design says that a Web page is more of a conduit for rich and social media content than a content vehicle in and of itself. But you can't expect bloggers and tweeters to find and post your rich media content if you don't also post it on the popular file sharing sites. Though many of these sites feature the *nofollow* attribute value on their links, many bloggers and other site owners frequent these sites looking for relevant, interesting content to complement their blogs or other posts. If they pick up your content, their link to your site will pass link juice.

The designers of the Web—the W3C, which is still led by Tim Berners-Lee after all these years—have developed technologies to extend the language of the Web and automate content publishing in the process. One such technology is colloquially called **Really Simple Syndication** (**RSS**). RSS lets you automatically distribute your content to people who have subscribed to it. So, if your content changes, your audience will be notified.

Rather than needing to check back on your site in case content changes, they can wait for RSS to update them and only click in when you post new stuff.

A more valuable aspect of RSS is how it allows two site owners to share content without touching it. Suppose you have a daily news section on your site and a colleague is interested in posting that same feed on his site. He can post the RSS code for your feed, and his site will be automatically filled with links to your fresh content, which users can access by clicking. If you can develop a relationship with a content partner who is willing to post a feed of your content on her site, you are in content nirvana. All those links will pass link juice to your pages. This might not be as hard as you think. For example, your business partners might want to post your feeds on their sites to ensure that their users get the most up-to-date information from their business partner company.

Summary

- Keywords mean different things in different contexts. To determine the context of a Web page, Google uses PageRank, which measures the quantity and quality of links into its content.

- On the Web, the value of content is directly proportional to how many links point to it.

- PageRank also is a measure of the authority of a site: The more links into a page, the more prominent it is on the Web.

- To become a hub of authority, look to Wikipedia as a model of publishing: Don't try to do too much, but engage with a community of subject matter experts who also own Web sites to produce a more complete content experience for the community's users.

- Use social media sites to engage with the community of like-minded subject matter experts and expand your network of connections.

- Don't expect to gain link juice directly from social media links, because most of those sites use the *nofollow* attribute.

- Even with the *nofollow* attribute, social media is the best way to gain indirect link juice, by publicizing content that might be relevant to your community and making it easy to link to it.

- Also consider posting rich media to file-sharing sites such as YouTube, iTunes, and SlideShare. Bloggers and others mine these sites for relevant videos, podcasts, and presentations.

- Use RSS feeds to help your audience subscribe to and share your content, thereby developing pass-along link juice.

CHAPTER   8

Capturing Social Media Opportunities

The Web is a social medium. As we showed in Chapter 7, the value of content on the Web is directly proportional to the quantity and quality of links to it. To get people to link to your content, you have to establish credibility with folks who share your interests and find your content compelling. To establish credibility, you have to develop relationships with them. Thus, if you hope to create valuable content on the Web, you must frequent the parts of the Web developed for social interaction and sharing. And it is not enough to merely lurk on these social sites. You must contribute. Providing quality social media contributions is a key differentiator between effective and ineffective Web communicators.

Throughout this book, we have used the lens of media determinism to try to distinguish Web communication from other types, especially print. (We defined media determinism in Chapter 2, but perhaps a refresher is in order. Media determinism is the view that what we communicate is at least in part determined by *the medium* in which we communicate. As Marshall McLuhan is famous for saying, "The medium is the message" [or massage].) The center of the distinction between Web and print writing is links. The social nature of the Web changes the way we write, not just from an information architecture perspective, but from a conceptual perspective. As we showed in Chapter 7, the concept of credibility is similar between print and Web. In both cases, you must get people to refer to your work in order for it to have value. But that is where the similarity ends: Unlike print publications, your Web pages cannot stand on their own. They must have the support of links between your content and complementary content. And that complementary content cannot be just within your domain. Some of those links must be between your domain and collaborators outside of it, in order for them to have sufficient value for Google and other search engines to give your content the visibility it needs. Without search engines ranking your content according to the links to it, your content will not be effective.

Some aspects of social media writing are common to all Web writing: Clear, concise, and compelling content that is relevant to the audience works, no matter where you are on the Web. But in social media, these values tend to be concentrated. In social media settings, clarity, conciseness, and persuasiveness aren't just values of good writing; they're necessities. On your own Web pages, a longer piece here or there might be effective for some members of your audience. But you would be utterly ineffective with a longer piece in Twitter, even if its character limit allowed for that. And in social media domains, you don't just address an anonymous audience of diverse visitors; you engage friends and followers with whom you have developed a relationship. Writing for those particular people requires an even tighter focus on what you want to say. This chapter delves into how and why good Web writing is ever more important in social media settings.

Retrievability—*how easy it is for your target audience to find your content*—is central to effective Web content. Nowhere is that more important than in social media settings. To make quality social media contributions, you must take advantage of the ways that social media sites use social tagging, visitor ratings, and other social applications to help users with similar interests find relevant content. Still, social media writing is not fundamentally different than writing in other parts of the Web. Effective writing for social media uses the same principles as the search-first writing methods we focused on in previous chapters. For example, writing effective copy so that users will tag it and rank it highly is very similar to writing effective copy for search engines. Here are some important points.

- **Social tagging is similar to keyword usage.** Social tags are words and phrases that users assign to content. Users can look for particular tags to find what is most relevant to them. Social tagging applications display tagged content to users in innovative experiences such as tag clouds. Obviously, keywords are similar to social tags. They also use words to describe content. Less obviously, perhaps, keywords can also be used in a social way. Search engines pull content related to the keyword clouds that writers use in their content. But writers use particular keywords to attract traffic from folks who are interested in them. Also, when you link to another site, you write the anchor text for those links. Google and Bing pay a lot of attention to the anchor text to assign relevance to links. In this sense, keywords are assigned by the linking sites, just like social tags.

  The main difference between social tagging and keyword usage is the person who assigns them to a piece of content. Writers assign keywords to their content. Readers typically assign tags to it. Also, unlike keywords, user tags are displayed onscreen, while search engines use "invisible" keywords to find relevant content to display. Still, the concept of writing with keywords placed in strategic places applies to social Web sites, just as much as it does to your own domain. If you use keywords appropriately, your content is more likely to be tagged by your readers. And when you tag your own content, keywords are the best place to start.

  Figure 8.1 shows an example of social tagging at Delicious.com.

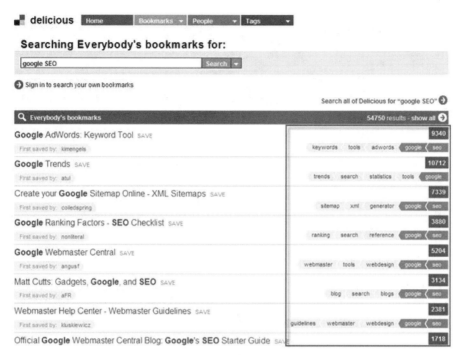

Figure 8.1   An example of social tagging in action at Delicious.com. The social tags are listed on the right of the screen shot, with a red box around them. Users can organize their bookmarked content by the tags they assign and share them with like-minded friends.

- User ratings are similar to links. Both links and user ratings are votes of confidence for content. But it's easier for users to vote for content they like using user ratings, because it is a one-click operation. Linking to content is decidedly not a one-click procedure. It often requires at least copying and pasting the link, writing the anchor text, and publishing the content with the link in it. Still, the concept of writing link bait applies in social media settings, just as it does on your own Web domain. Link bait is just highly credible content, whether it appears on your domain or elsewhere. In social media settings, it is more likely to be highly rated. For search engines, links are votes for content. On social sites, "diggs" or "likes" are votes of confidence for content. Perhaps links are better indicators of the perceived quality of content, because of the level of difficulty in "voting" with links rather than by clicking the **digg** button on Digg.com. But the concept is the same.

    Figure 8.2 shows an example of user ratings at Digg.com.

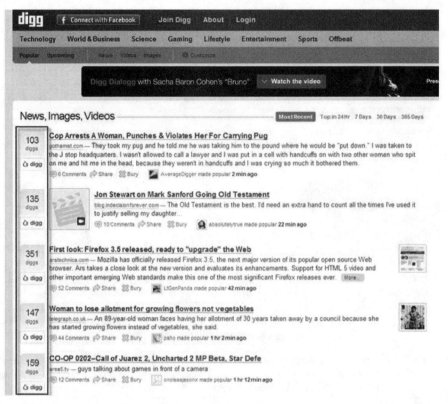

Figure 8.2   An example of user ratings at Digg.com. Users can click the "digg" link highlighted in the red box to indicate that they like the content. Users will tend to click more often on more popular content.

Some bloggers who write about writing for social media seem to think that social media is very different from ordinary Web writing. Contrary to what we say, these writers claim that some of the basic principles of good Web content don't apply to social media. For example, Walter Pike writes the following:

> Social media is different. It's different because the reader is in control and the reader is cynical and doesn't trust spin and brand speak. The reader will participate and comment and, because he or she is connected, will share his or her views with their network. To some it may be bad news but social media is not a fad and it is here to stay. (*Source:* www.bizcommunity.com/Article/196/16/25990.html)

First of all, we agree with the last line: Social media is here to stay. We expect it to only grow in popularity as time goes on. We also agree that in social media settings, the reader is in control, is cynical, and wants to participate. What we don't agree with is that these readers' practices are unique to social media. As we have been claiming throughout this book, the Web as a whole is different from print because Web readers are in control and are more skeptical than print readers. That may be somewhat heightened in social media settings, but it is common in more traditional Web sites. Even before discussing social media, we have encouraged you to enable reader feedback and ratings and other ways for readers to interact with your content. You can do those things just as well on your site as the social media applications do. Yes, social media is here to stay. But social media experiences are not (or should not be) fundamentally different than the Web experiences on your domain. Actually, the only thing we would change about the above quotation is to replace the words "social media" with "Web content."

Some bloggers take the attitude that writing for social media is different than Web writing to extremes. At www.copyblogger.com/writing-for-social-media, Muhammad Saleem says:

> The social media everyman is looking for an entertaining diversion, while being receptive to learning something new if presented in an "edutainment" format that ties the lesson into popular culture.

In the same post as above, he recommends the following headlines for blog posts, which had appeared earlier on copyblogger.com:

- Did Alanis Morissette Get Irony Right?
- The David Lee Roth Guide to Legendary Marketing
- What Owen Wilson's Pursed Lips Mean to Your Blog
- Don't Be Cameron Diaz
- What Prince Can Teach You About Effective Blogging

These headlines could not be in more direct conflict with our advice in this book. What's wrong with them? First of all, just because you're writing a blog, you shouldn't throw away everything we taught you about writing descriptive headings that contain the keywords your target audience uses. Users who search on these celebrity names, click through to the results, and land on one of these blog posts, unaware that the blog is actually about writing for blogs, will instantly bounce. Every bounce is a bad user experience and a negative influence on your credibility.

Search is the universal application on the Web, whether the site is a blog or a traditional Web site. All the techniques that we described in Chapters 4 and 5 apply in social settings as well. If anything, they are even *more* important in social settings, because you have less space in which to do search optimization. Spamming a heading or title tag with irrelevant keywords is wrong everywhere on the Web.

Second, content transparency is central to writing link bait. If you try to pump up traffic volume with misleading headings, no credible source will take you seriously. Using celebrity names to drive traffic to your blog posts is akin to metadata spamming. Search engines will not be the only sites to boot you from their lists of credible sources if you pull tricks like this.

Also, Saleem misses the point of Web audience analysis. The study he cites as suggesting using an "edutainment" format was conducted on a cross section of Web users, some of whom, undoubtedly, cared about the entertainment industry. If your users don't care about the entertainment industry, using an "edutainment" technique will only turn them off to what might otherwise be good content.

Saleem also cites the study "The Latest Headlines—Your Vote Counts" from journalism .org (http://www.journalism.org/node/7493). However, this study actually comes to radically different conclusions than Saleem seems to think it does. It says that when users vote on content that they find interesting or important in social settings, their votes are highly diverse. In contrast to the mainstream media, they don't focus on one topic—such as the death of Michael Jackson—to the exclusion of others. In particular, when the mainstream media seems to fixate on one story related to celebrities, the social networks are off taking deeper dives into all sorts of diverse interests in news around the globe. So, far from suggesting that you use the same words or celebrity names as the mainstream press in your social media headlines and tweets, the study suggests that you ignore those words and use ones that connect with the particular needs of your audience.

We cannot emphasize enough just how wrong Saleem is here. If you use the techniques we have outlined in previous chapters and later in this chapter to write relevant content for your Web audiences, you will succeed. These techniques work in both overt social settings and in the less obvious social setting of your own Web domain. Here's a quick refresher.

- Learn the content needs of your target audience, and use words and phrases relevant to those needs.
- Write your content, starting with the keywords that your target audience members use in their own content efforts (such as search queries, tweets, and blog posts).
- Link in an intelligent way to the most credible content related to your topic, rather than replicating what is already published on the Web.
- Use your own voice to create original content that complements the ongoing conversation on the Web; but only write if you have something original and credible to say.
- Collaborate with credible sources that you have found, to weave your original content into the body of work on a topic, encouraging links from their content into yours.

Social media is a catch-all phrase that is used to describe a variety of Web content models and user interface applications, not all of which fit neatly in any one category. For this reason, beyond our generic advice in previous chapters, our advice regarding writing for social media is geared toward the particular content models and user interface applications within social sites. For example, writing for Twitter is very different than writing for Facebook, though some of the same principles apply.

Social media sites are evolving, and new ones crop up every day. So it is impossible to be all-inclusive in a book such as this. Rather than treating each existing social media site here (that could be the subject of a whole network of sites or series of books), we will focus on a few of the main ones and leave the definitive social media writing guide to some other effort. Applications on which we focus include forums, wikis, blogs, microblogs (such as Twitter pages), and persona sites (such as Facebook and LinkedIn). Other social media sites, such as MySpace, Xing, Google Wave, and Windows Live Spaces, will be left to follow-on work on this book's companion blog, http://writingfordigital.com.

> Social media domains are just sophisticated extensions of the Web. Each domain tries to solve the same problem that search engines have been trying to solve for the general Web: How do you enable Web users to find, share, and consume Web content that is relevant to their interests?

Listening: How to Use Social Media to Better Understand Your Audience's Vocabulary

Social media not only helps users find relevant content; it can also help you understand the language of the conversations used by your target audience. The practice of mining social media sites for information on audience nomenclature is called **listening**. Listening encompasses several areas of social media market intelligence research, including sentiment analysis and various forms of semantic analysis of tags, posts, and bookmarks in social media settings. See Chapter 5 for more detailed information about listening tools and methods.

Though we cover this in detail in Chapter 5, we can't emphasize enough the value of using social media to learn how your target audience writes. The words they use to describe and tag things are the same words they use in search engine queries. So your social media listening can help you define your target audience in terms of their views and insights. This will help you attract them to conversations on your site, by using the words and phrases they use. Once they come to your site, you can use these conversations to inform and persuade them. In this way, social media becomes a powerful force of thought leadership and change among the community of people who comprise your sphere of influence.

Forums: The Original Online Communities

Forums have been around since before the Web even existed. Before the Web, they resembled online bulletin boards where like-minded users could share information about their passions. For example, when one of the authors of this book (James Mathewson) was in graduate school, he participated in a forum called Rhetlist (now available on the Web at http://blog.lib.umn.edu/logie/rhetlist/), which served a community of educators and scholars interested in the rhetoric of print and online media. At the time, users didn't come to Rhetlist through the (not-yet-born) Web, but through an online system administered by the University of Minnesota. Almost every academic discipline had a series of forums and discussion lists similar to Rhetlist.

Forums were also adopted by businesses to promote products and enable users to help each other resolve issues with the products. Often, these product-related forums were independent of the vendors themselves and were instead affiliated with **Special Interest Groups (SIGs)** related to a product or product family. Members of SIGs (which were also known as **user groups**), often met face to face in addition to participating in the SIGs online. Today, SIGs and other types of user groups still exist, much as they have for the past quarter century, with or without vendor sponsorship.

Among other things, forums were (and are) informal "spaces" where participants:

- Share "inside" information with peers and colleagues
- Form relationships with potential collaborators
- Bounce ideas off of peers prior to publication
- Promote and extend existing publications

Though forums now use the Web as a wrapper application, the basic principles for writing in forums are the same now as they were 25 years ago. First of all, forums are often moderated. Without moderation, participants can veer off topic. Because forums are intended to have a rather narrow topical scope, writers of irrelevant content are often censured, and their work is deleted. Repeated violations can get participants banned from a forum. In today's blog community sites, participants are also expected to stay "on topic," though moderation is typically less stringent.

Second, forums are somewhat more insular than a blog community site. New users are encouraged to "lurk" for awhile to get a sense of the topicality of a forum, and its style. After a user has posted fairly regularly, moderators give her more leeway about what she may post. So, for example, you might see an occasional off-topic post by a regular forum participant. When new posters see these off-topic posts, they get the idea that the forum is not tightly moderated, and will sometimes write an off-topic post. When they do this, they are often severely censured.

On forums, it takes quite a few good posts to gain the credibility of the whole community. Before crossing that threshold of credibility, posters must be judicious in contributing. In this regard, writing for forums is similar to other social media venues: The community must show its acceptance of you by responding to your posts with positive comments. Until you have that credibility, your work within forums is limited primarily to reading and making short positive comments on topics. This can be frustrating for those who have important things to say, but whose personas are still relatively unknown. For this reason, building your persona can be as important as writing strong content. Gaining credibility or reputation involves a combination of your body of work and your persona. Your goal in forums is to build that credibility—otherwise known as your reputation.

Of course, credibility is also a common currency in social media settings (and in the Web in general). On the Web, before you can be effective, you need to develop credibility with your audience, and especially with others in your field who will link to your content. In conventional Web sites, it's a bit more difficult to know when you have the needed credibility. (We showed in Chapter 7 that this is best measured by search visibility and referrals.) In social media settings, you have direct anecdotal evidence of your credibility by the sentiment of the comments that engage with your posts. So credibility might be easier to gauge in social media contexts. But either way, it is a bellwether of Web effectiveness. When you have credibility, all the metrics that we describe in Chapter 9 will start to go in your favor, indicating Web effectiveness.

Wikis: The Purest Form of Web Content

As we mentioned in Chapter 7, Wikipedia is a model for how we recommend that content teams should manage their content, whether within wikis or in other areas. It is very similar to what Tim Berners-Lee envisioned when he developed the Web at CERN: a team of experts collaborating on related content in real time. Somehow, that vision got lost as corporate interests tried to create the Web in the image of print, and to use it as a transaction engine, with good success. But Wikipedia brought back the ideal of the Web as an information management application. It has shown over time the true power of the Web. Wikipedia works by engaging subject matter experts on every conceivable topic and using an army of volunteer editors to ensure the accuracy and completeness of the topics. The integrity of the content process and the credibility of the experts engaged in the project ultimately resulted in Wikipedia taking the top position in Google for hundreds of thousands of keywords.

Of course, Wikipedia is only one of thousands of wikis on the Web. It is just the most comprehensive and recognizable one. Organizations large and small are using wikis as a way to connect internal and external experts on topics of interest. At IBM, for example, we have wikis related to most of our product lines. Because they engage the community in a transparent way, wikis are the fastest growing kind of content in the ibm.com domain in terms of traffic volumes. They also are drawing search traffic away from some of our more traditional marketing pages on the same topics. This challenge is being met by ensuring that the wikis link to traditional Web pages. In this way, we can capture some link juice while providing an interactive form of content to our target audience.

Wikis are not only great vehicles of content for companies, but for individuals as well. If you are an expert on a topic, it is worth your while to try to get content published on Wikipedia related to that topic. To do this, start by commenting on the existing content on that topic and see if you can get approval to fill holes or gaps, as needed. Wikipedia is always looking for helpers to make it an even better free reference. Once you have some content up on Wikipedia, you can link to it and use it as a way to promote your credibility on the topic in other venues, such as your blog or Twitter page.

Wikipedia is not the only place where good writers can make a name for themselves. You can create your own wiki environment on your site, using free tools such as Wetpaint (www.wetpaint.com). These are good ways to publish content that needs frequent updates and regular collaboration from team members who share a topic area. Be careful, though. Because wikis are live environments, they are susceptible to higher error rates. And they can be vandalized, so you'll need to do daily maintenance. Because of this, they are not necessarily the best option for content that will persist on your environment. But for quick updates around a shell of topics, wikis are great avenues in which to more fully engage with your target audience.

Writing for wikis is somewhat different than writing for Web pages, because you serve as your own architect. You decide when to make a new page within a topic and how to populate it. Unlike more traditional Web environments, where templates typically enforce strict character counts, wikis are much more flexible, expanding and contracting to fit the topic at hand. That said, the temptation is to become overly verbose if you have more room to work with. So you must still write concisely, keeping in mind that Web readers scan before reading and skim otherwise, especially if topics are on the long side.

We said earlier that wikis are the purest form of Web publishing because they fit Tim Berners-Lee's original Web concept. But there are other reasons. For one thing, wikis are uncomplicated from the standpoint of code and metadata. It is almost impossible to be anything but transparent in them. So our advice about writing genuine link bait by starting with keywords that resonate with your target audience should be a natural consequence of writing for wikis, provided that you learn what your target audience needs. They're also places that rely heavily on links—not only internal to the wiki, but to external resources. For this reason, link juice is a natural consequence of good wiki architecture. Wikipedia is a great example of how to own topics on thousands of keywords in Google without even trying to do SEO. The integrity of the process virtually ensures it.

Blogging to Grow Your Voice

Blogs are topic-centric sites in which personalities write regular Web columns and encourage participation with regular readers. Blog formats are about as diverse as Web sites, so it makes little sense to form a narrow definition here. But, in addition to conventional Web writing best practices, there are a few features that all blogs have in common, which affect blog best practices.

- Like Web sites, the most successful blogs look for gaps in subject matter. If you find yourself saying the same thing as other more established bloggers, consider a new niche.

- Blogs are personality-driven. As with a column in a newspaper, the writer's voice and reputation are as important as what he or she writes about in a given day.

- Unlike some Web content, the expectation is for blogs to be updated with fresh content regularly. Most readers will subscribe to your blog using RSS. If they aren't notified about a new post very often, they might stop clicking through to your blog.

- Also, blogs have regular followers who comment—often multiple times a day—and interact with each other in the comment section. Regular blog commenters can be an important source of interest for your readers.

Each of these aspects of blogs changes the way we think about writing for them. We will delve more deeply into each here.

Find your niche. The easiest way to develop a loyal audience is to provide unique content. Just as you would lurk in a forum (hang out without commenting) and figure out what is both topical and as yet unsaid, follow the blogs on your topic of interest and find out what they're *not* talking about. Then fill that gap. Of course, you want to acknowledge how important your work is relative to theirs and develop all kinds of links between your content and theirs. The more tightly you integrate with other experts, the more effective your blog will be.

Unveil your personality. Perhaps the single most important thing about a blog is to bring out your own personality. Building in an occasional personal reference can endear you to your audience. In some cases, even if the personal reference isn't endearing, it helps to be a somewhat crusty character. Don't tell your whole story right away or inundate your audience with personal anecdotes. But an occasional personal reference can strengthen the personal connection you develop with your audience.

Keep it fresh. Try to find something to say regularly (we recommend at least weekly), even if once in a while you have a short post or a regular post of all the links you've discovered over the course of a week. If you don't give your audience a reason to come to your page weekly, they will get out of the habit of coming to your site.

Cultivate comments. In a blog, readers' comments are almost as important as the posts themselves. Regular posters will respond to each other and drive the comments up considerably. There's no secret to getting people to comment, but it helps to take risks and purposely be controversial. Controversy breeds comments, which lead to more comments. You can have accurate, unique content and it won't gain many comments because there's nothing to disagree with. But if you make a few bold statements, some will respond to the controversy and the battle lines will be drawn. Nothing does more to develop a loyal following than to see lively debates in your comment section.

Enable linkbacks. Some blog software, such as WordPress, allows you to track when and where people link to your blog posts. *Linkbacks* come in several varieties—most notably *trackbacks* and *pingbacks*, which are often colloquially referred to as *trackbacks*. Linkbacks are valuable because they help you monitor the conversation around your writing, and in some cases, engage with those who link to your work to establish a richer content relationship with their work.

The technical details of trackbacks and pingbacks are somewhat complex and outside the scope of this book. If you enable linkbacks on your blog, you will need to carefully manage the spam that inevitably arises from them. Spam bots follow links through the blogosphere to find places to post automated marketing messages, which dilute the effectiveness of your comments. Both types of linkbacks—trackbacks and pingbacks—require you to monitor, delete, and block spammers from using your comment section as a place to tout their nefarious products and services. The extra management effort is well worth it, however, because link information is some of the most important data you can receive about your blog. Linkbacks enable you to monitor and take action and improve your blog's link equity.

Optimizing Your Blog for Search

Optimizing blogs for search is very similar to optimizing conventional Web pages. You have to get your keywords into titles, headings, URLs, and link anchor text. You have to write concise content packed with the most relevant keywords and their semantic derivatives. And you have to aggressively develop linking relationships with other blogs on similar topics. There are some unique aspects of optimizing your blog for search, however, which are worth noting:

- **Ping your blog.** Because your blog is updated regularly, the crawler can often be behind the freshest post by at least a day. To speed that process up, it's a good idea to use Ping-o-Matic (Figure 8.3) to notify other sites of a new post so they can index and aggregate content. Other ping sites include KingPing and Google Blog Search. You can also use the *autoping* function, which does as the name suggests, saving you the effort of pinging your posts yourself.

- **Optimize your RSS feeds.** Really Simple Syndication (RSS) is a great way to get the word out on regularly updated content. Among other things, RSS lets your audience subscribe to notices of new content, so they only need to come to your site when they know the content is fresh. Because RSS feeds are crawled and indexed by Google, RSS is also a great way to let Google know about your content. The actual RSS feeds can be optimized like short blog posts, using the most relevant keywords in strategic places, especially titles and headings.

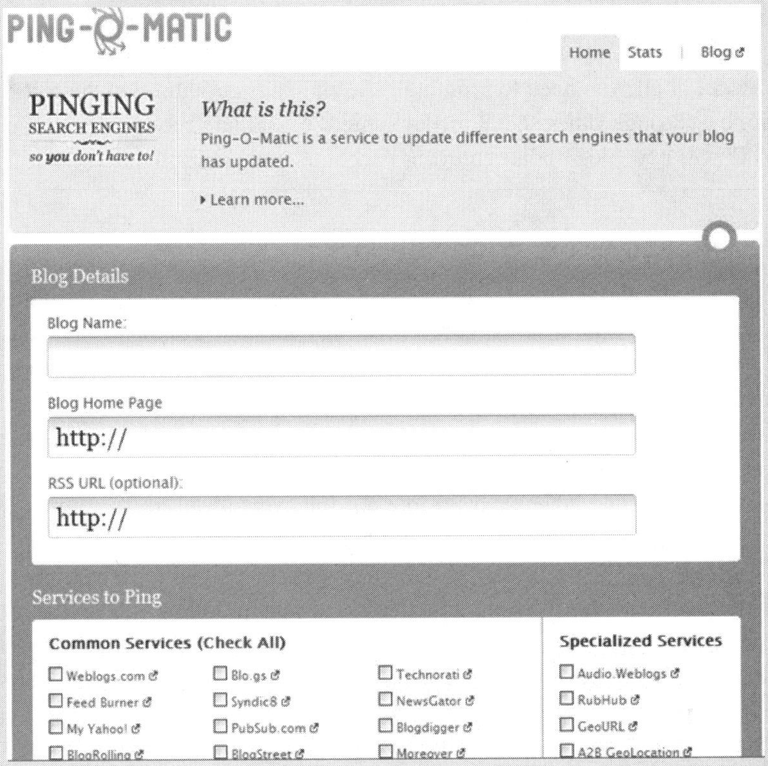

Figure 8.3 Ping-o-Matic lets you ping your content to more than a dozen blog sites.

In blog contexts, the best way to enable RSS is to add the following code to the header of each page of your blog:

```
<link rel="alternate" type="application/rss+xml" href
=http://www.example.com/ title="Great example blog (RSS)"
/>
```

- **Spread the word.** Use social tagging to help your audience, and search engines, determine the relevance of a blog post to a topic. Because your audience tags the content, tags are an accurate way of determining what words your audience finds relevant to your posts. These social tags also let you optimize your links to your content to Digg, Delicious, and other social sites with the assigned tags. Getting your blog listed on these sites, and enabling your audience to assign tags to it and pass it around, are the best ways to grow an audience of regular visitors and contributors.

A blog is a big commitment. To do it right, you must be prepared to post something weekly. You need to monitor comments and occasionally respond to a commenter. Be prepared to moderate the comments section and remove spam whenever you find it. Perhaps most important of all, you need to promote your blog, not only through the tactics we outline above, but through other social media venues. Tweet and retweet your blog posts on Twitter. And post new blog updates on your Facebook and LinkedIn pages.

Using Twitter to Grow Your Network

Twitter is a microblogging site that lets users develop a following of folks with common interests. You develop that following by "tweeting" valuable commentary about areas of expertise. People search on keywords in your tweets and eventually follow you because of their interests in those keywords, and especially your reputation in the field.

At the time of writing, Twitter has a low signal-to-noise ratio. By that we mean that a high percentage of Twitter users don't really get the concept and tweet on things of little interest to their followers. The more tweets from your followers about irrelevant things, the less useful the application is. Your followers can choose to stop following you if you post too much noise. So developing a loyal group of followers forces you to tighten your focus on your area of expertise so that those interested in it will want to follow you, within reason. Just as with your blog, we recommend folding in an occasional personal item of interest to build your persona with your followers. The more followers you have, the bigger your sphere of influence. That sphere of influence is a good measure of your credibility, and an excellent way to promote your content in other Web venues, such as your blog and your Web site.

One of the reasons Twitter users struggle with the application is the strict 140-character limit for tweets. If you try to post a tweet with more than 140 characters, the application will tell you to be more concise. Saying something worth posting in fewer than 140 characters (letters, spaces, and punctuation marks) is a difficult challenge for writers accustomed to having as much space as they need to say what they want. There are three responses to this:

1. You can refrain from tweeting because you can't seem to find the words to say your piece concisely.

2. You can feel compelled to write something insignificant or irrelevant because it fits into the 140-character limit and you feel the pressure to tweet daily.

3. You can take on the challenge of saying important things in the space provided.

The first response will reduce your roster of followers, as they assume you don't have anything interesting to say on a regular basis. The second response will cause you to lose followers who grow weary of weeding through noise to get to the signals. The third response will lead to you gain followers. Because Twitter success is measured by the number of followers you have, we will focus on techniques of fitting your insights into the space provided. Optimizing those tweets is a further step that we will cover below.

As Twitter gains popularity, it will change the way people write on the Web. A strict space constraint forces writers to be more concise about every aspect of their writing. They learn to cut needless words out of sentences. They learn to write with more verbs and fewer adjectives. They learn to write in active voice. In short, they learn all the lessons they need to write more concisely in all their Web work, and increase their effectiveness for Web audiences.

First and foremost, concise writing demands that you don't try to say too much in your tweets. One single thought is all you need. If you have other related thoughts, you can always say them in subsequent tweets. Some writers struggle to reduce their thinking down to elemental insights and focus on one per tweet. If you find yourself really struggling to fit your insight into a tweet, consider breaking it up into two related insights.

Second, you'd be surprised how few words it takes to write a single insight if you edit your work down to size. A good reference for how to do this is Strunk and White's *Elements of Style* (1979, 23-4). For example, one very common phrase is *due to the fact that*; it can be simply replaced with *because*. Another common problem is putting the adjective at the end of the sentence, although it's shorter and punchier to put it before the noun. We won't go into all of the habits of concise writing here. Repeatedly editing your own work will eventually teach you to say more important things with fewer words.

You can reduce the character count in your tweets with some of the application's functions.

- Use a URL shortener, such as bit.ly (http://bit.ly/) to rewrite the URLs you embed into your posts with the fewest possible characters.

- Use the @ sign before a follower's Twitter name to show that you are responding to a tweet by one of your followers. This lets you get right to the point of the tweet.

- Use the hashtag (#) function to indicate keyword tags in your tweets. This not only lets you condense your writing by breaking it into its most elemental keywords, but it will help you follow threads of content between tweets. Simply follow @hashtags to have your hashtags tracked. You can follow your hashtags in real time at hashtags.org.

Hashtags are one way to optimize your tweets for search engines, including the Twitter search engine. But they should be used judiciously. Choose hashtags as you would keywords on Web pages: one per page or tweet. Your hashtags should also be part of the network of keyword clouds surrounding your area of expertise. Using keywords and hashtags based on popularity, rather than on relevance to your area of expertise, is akin to spamming. You can attract a lot of followers who are not directly interested in your tweets, and thereby damage your image in the process. Or you can turn off your followers by using hashtags that are not relevant to their interests.

One of the best ways to measure the success of your tweets is by the number of *retweets*, or tweets that other users embed in their own tweets. Because retweets typically contain a link to the original tweet, they also improve link equity to your twitter page. In his research on the subject, coauthor Frank Donatone discovered several ways to improve the chances that your tweets will get retweeted. Here are the highlights of that research.

- **Time of day.** If you tweet during normal business hours (EST), you will have a better chance of getting retweeted. You can use the tweetlater function (www .tweetlater.com/) to automate your tweet timing.
- **Links.** Tweets with links in them are three times more likely to get retweeted.
- **Self reference.** If your tweets are related to how twitter affects your area of expertise, they will be more likely to get retweeted.
- **Timeliness.** If you are the first among your followers to tweet on a timely topic, it will be more likely to get retweeted among your followers.

Twitter is a great way to tighten your focus on your target audience by attracting like-minded followers and promoting your content to them. Writing concise, search-optimized tweets is an emerging art form. But the same principles that govern successful SEO in other Web venues apply.

- Use search-optimized titles
- Constrain tweets to one insight
- Tweet in the fewest possible words
- Use a URL shortener, such as bit.ly
- Add a relevant hashtag
- Work to get retweets

If you do these things, you will grow your following and maximize the value of your time spent on Twitter.

Optimizing Your Facebook and LinkedIn Presences

We don't advocate using Twitter to build your online character. There is little room for writing personal tweets to people who are following your professional persona. For hobbies and other passions outside of your professional persona, we advocate using Facebook. For more involved professional news about you than you can tweet, we recommend LinkedIn.

Facebook is a site that enables you to build a personal profile comprising your full range of interests. It replicates what early Web users tried to do on their own: build a site that encapsulates your values, projects, tastes, friends, and family. You develop a network of friends, who alone can see your posts and poll responses (if you manage your security settings appropriately). And you write short daily posts that call attention to the best examples of these aspects of your character.

LinkedIn is another venue to get your name out there. While Facebook is primarily a place to connect with friends and family, LinkedIn is primarily a place to cultivate professional contacts. There will be some overlap between your LinkedIn connections and your Facebook friends, so the distinction is not sharp. But if you think of the two as serving somewhat different purposes, you can channel your messages to one or the other depending on purpose. For example, if you have an important publication that you want your professional contacts to know about, post an update to your LinkedIn page. If you did something fun or interesting in your personal life, post it to Facebook. Of course you can cross post and even set up feeds from Twitter to Facebook and LinkedIn. But managing three pages and a blog with the kind of intensity that folks display on Twitter can consume more of your time than you have, and you will end up not being able to say anything interesting about yourself.

The value of your Facebook or LinkedIn personas is that they are about trust. If you help your friends and connections understand the breadth and depth of your character and experience, they are more likely to trust your writing in other settings. Of course, both sites are also great places to collaborate and connect with your network. Forming and participating in groups is an essential way to grow your network of friends and connections beyond those you formed through past and present companies you worked for. Actions speak louder than words. Collaborating with friends and connections gives you an opportunity to directly demonstrate that the persona you promote on Facebook and LinkedIn accurately represents what you're about.

Of course, Facebook and LinkedIn are also great places to promote your Web writing. They enable you to post links to your blog or Web sites when new updates are available. As mentioned, both Facebook and LinkedIn allow auto feed from Twitter (using the `#fb` and `#in` hashtags), so that your tweets can be automatically posted on your Facebook and LinkedIn pages for all your friends and professional connections to see. When Twitter followers become Facebook friends or LinkedIn connections, this lets you show that your professional and personal personas are compatible, or even integrated.

Writing in these settings poses some unique challenges. As with Twitter, shorter posts tend to be more effective. Facebook posts with links tend to get reposted by others. Cultivating and writing in your voice is particularly effective when you know your audience well and they know you well. Using the conversational tone that you cultivate in your blog will get more comments than bland or flat text. Finally, although your blog won't get direct link juice from these mentions, promoting your blog to other bloggers through Twitter, Facebook, and LinkedIn is the surest way to get them to link to your blog posts. As on other Web venues, link equity is the surest way to drive targeted traffic to your Web content, especially your blog.

At times, Facebook and LinkedIn are less about writing than they are about posting links to videos, photos, and other rich media assets. Sometimes you can say more with rich media than you can with text. For these times, using Facebook and LinkedIn to make your point is the most effective way to connect with your friends and contacts.

Sustainable Practices for the Web as a Social Medium

As we have mentioned, it takes a big commitment to thrive in social media. The temptation is to try to push your name out there and get a lot of friends and followers in a hurry. You can do this, but it might not be the best strategy. Too often, people come to social sites with a lot of energy and later find that they can't sustain their initial enthusiasm. They get burned out on the daily activities and their blogs, Twitter pages, and Facebook pages are suddenly thin on content.

A lifeless blog with irregular posts is worse than no blog at all. Followers and commenters will stop coming to your social venues when you do not provide regular updates. For this reason, we recommend starting small with a blog, moving to Facebook and LinkedIn pages, and eventually creating a Twitter page. If you gradually ramp up to a rich complement of venues, you can sustain success.

If you take a realistic look at how much time you can devote to the four primary social venues (blogs, Facebook, LinkedIn, and Twitter), you can develop an integrated social media strategy. The general strategy uses your Web page for persistent content, your blog for daily insights, your Twitter page for condensed insights, and your Facebook and LinkedIn pages for your persona.

A general sustainable content strategy also means not trying to do too much in terms of the topics you focus on. As we showed in Chapter 7, the object is to become a hub of authority on subjects for which you are considered an expert; that prospect depends on making connections with other experts in your field, and rather than trying to compete with them, collaborating with them. Find the white space in their work and fill it with original insights and research. Become the connection point in their work. When you apply this overarching goal to the four social media venues we talk about in this chapter, your task won't seem so overwhelming.

You will have more success by defining your scope as a hub of authority, where the spokes are your Web audience, blog commenters, Facebook friends, LinkedIn contacts, and Twitter followers. By not trying to own every topic, but letting collaborators do their work and promoting it on your social media venues, your collaborators will give you the credit you deserve in the form of links, and Google will rank your content with the visibility it deserves.

Summary

- The Web is a social medium.
- Social sites such as blogs, Facebook, and Twitter are just more overtly social than traditional Web pages.
- Social media innovations such as social tags and ratings are similar to keywords and links, respectively.
- Blogging is similar to writing for the Web, except that it's much more focused on a single topic and on a well-defined audience.
- Pinging, RSS feeds, and participation in social tagging sites are keys to blogging success and SEO.
- Twitter can extend your blog reach by developing a rich group of like-minded followers.
- Facebook can enhance your blog and Twitter persona by letting your friends know about your side projects, values, tastes, friends, and family.
- Integrating the content you publish to these four venues can help you develop a sustainable content model that extends your connections with collaborators.

CHAPTER 9

Measuring Web Content Effectiveness

If you publish a book such as this, you know that you can't make changes until the next printing, which might not be for six months to a year. So you have to try to write content with a long shelf life. Our goal is to write content that will remain relevant and current until the next printing. Small fluctuations in the field, such as which social media sites are hot right now, must be left to other content efforts, preferably on the Web, where daily changes can be made. Also, we have made every effort to write for our target audience—writers, editors, and content strategists—in this book. We expect to get reader feedback that tells us how well we did in that task and where we have room for improvement. But we can't make those improvements until the next printing. Again, our Web site—www.writingfordigital .com—will have to serve as a proxy for those adjustments until the next printing.

Indeed, one of the great advantages of Web publishing over print is the ability to improve content experiences as often as you want. This is not just about whether something is accurate, clean, or clear. It's about what is relevant. If you find that your audience is behaving unexpectedly on your site, you can change the content or design to better adapt to audience behavior. In this way, you make your site more effective for the audience that finds your content relevant. That is a practice we have been preaching throughout this book.

But how do you measure user behavior? There are many tools to help you do this. Every team needs a tool box of Web analytics tools—such as Unica NetInsight. Which set of tools you choose depends on your environment. Tool recommendations are beyond the scope of this chapter. What we want to do is explain the data you can gather with the various analytics tools and how to interpret it and use it to improve your content.

How do you interpret users' behavior in ways that help you improve your Web experiences for them? That is the subject of this chapter. In the typical environment, content strategists, writers, and editors don't need to conduct Web analytics. That's left to specialists. Rather than delving into how to gather the data (something best left to a book just about Web analytics), we want to help our target audience understand the range of possibilities, so that they can work with Web analytics specialists to pull, analyze, and interpret the data. In your roles as content strategists, writers, and editors, you will need to work with

147

Web analytics people to request reports and optimize dashboards. Knowing what data to request and how to use it to improve your content is the focus of this chapter.

Tools like Unica NetInsight can help you gather a wide array of data; listing all of it here is counterproductive. Instead, we'll start with the information that is most helpful for understanding Web content effectiveness. This will act as a filter that you can use to determine the right mix of analysis to request. Armed with the right analysis, you can better understand how users are interacting with your content and make improvements accordingly. Because this book defines Web content effectiveness in terms of the degree to which your content is relevant to the target audience, we will focus on measurements that can help you create more relevant content for your audience.

Note: Web analytics is a mixture of objective and subjective judgments. Tools can help you understand raw data, but how you interpret that data is often up to you. In particular, you must define for yourself the criteria that you use for relevance. For example, you might say that your goal for relevance for your audience is fifty percent engagement, meaning that half of the users who come to your page will engage with it. Depending on the purpose of your page, that goal can be quite reasonable. But for some contexts, it is not.

Suppose that you define engagement for your blog as having users make lots of comments on your posts. It is highly unusual to get fifty percent of your blog readers to comment—two percent is a good goal there. If you still want to demonstrate that half your visitors find your blog relevant (a very attainable goal) you will have to measure relevance more broadly, say by measuring time on a page, repeat visits, or RSS subscriptions. But this data doesn't mean anything unless you put an interpretive framework around it. How you do that is up to you. We will merely suggest helpful interpretive frameworks to use in your work with Web analytics professionals.

Measuring Engagement, Inferring Relevance

We will start by discussing how to measure user behavior in ways that give us insights into content relevance. Aside from asking your users if they find your content relevant (as we do in some pages in ibm.com), assessing relevance is a matter of measuring user engagement with your content and inferring relevance from those measurements.

A quick refresher on relevance is in order (see Chapter 3 for a more thorough discussion). Again, there is no direct measurement of relevance. It must be measured by inference, in both online and offline contexts, such as print.

For example, we infer the relevance of single-word utterances such as "pizza?" based on facts about the context external to the actual language—such as time, place, and who is speaking. Suppose this is said by a colleague with whom you eat lunch every day at different restaurants. And suppose he says it at 11:45 a.m. while standing in your office door. The context is so thoroughly determined that you can clearly infer its relevance: He wants you to join him for lunch at the pizza place. But the same utterance, coming at random from a stranger on a crowded street, is gibberish. In other words, lacking contextual cues from which to infer relevance, you deem the stranger's utterance to be totally irrelevant. Of course, there is a range of cases between these two that display some degree of relevance. (We leave it to the reader to think of examples.)

Assessing relevance in everyday life is part and parcel of learning language. But on the Web, it is not second nature. On the Web, we learn to focus on certain cues to determine the relevance of content. According to Nielsen (2008) and others, most Web users are savvy enough to do this within a few seconds. If they determine that a page is irrelevant, they will leave it within a few seconds. If they determine that it's at least marginally relevant, they will spend more time on it and perhaps engage more deeply with it by clicking calls to action.

> The more a user engages with a page, the more relevant he or she finds it. That is the primary assumption with which we infer relevance by measuring user engagement. A user engages with a page if she clicks a link on it.

Here are some ways you can measure your users' engagement and infer relevance from it.

- **Traffic.** Most discussions about Web analytics start with traffic data, typically defined in one of three ways:

    1. *Page views*—the number of times a page was viewed in a given time period.

    2. *Visits*, also known as *sessions*—the number of times your site was visited in a given period. This count includes multiple visits from the same user, who perhaps viewed multiple pages on your site.

    3. *Unique visits*—the number of individual users who came to your site in that time period.

    Page views are valuable because they can help you understand which pages in your site are hit more often. The other two main statistics are about visits to your site. Some combination of knowledge about visits and page views is necessary if you want to get a sense of the relative relevance of your pages to your overall site.

    Of the three, the *unique visits* stat is often considered the most valuable because it excludes users who keep coming back. However, some people like to measure *repeat visitors,* because that stat shows that your site has very high value for those users. If you get a lot of repeat visitors, you know the site's content is relevant for them. The number of repeat visitors also demonstrates visitor loyalty.

    The other stat some people use is *new visitors*—the number of visitors who have never visited your site before. This is not particularly helpful in measuring relevance. You can get a lot of new visitors who leave and never come back, which is an indication that those users find your content irrelevant.

Raw traffic data is not a good measure of relevance, in general, because it is possible that lots of people will land on your page and find it irrelevant and go away. Every time you force a user to use the **Back** button, you leave a negative impression on that user. The goal of Web content is not just to get a high volume of traffic, but to get *targeted* traffic. In short, you want to attract your target audience with relevant content.

- **Bounce rate.** The percentage of users who leave your site in a few seconds without clicking anything. This is defined in different ways, but the typical added assumption is that a "bounce" is not defined by failing to click a desired link right away. It's typically defined as clicking the **Back** button within a few seconds.

  Bounce rate is important because it measures the percentage of users who find your content irrelevant almost immediately. A high bounce rate indicates that you are getting traffic to your page that is not part of your target audience. Knowing a page's bounce rate can't help you diagnose the problem. But a high bounce rate is the first warning sign that the users coming to your page are not in your target audience.

  Most tools that measure traffic can measure clicks: Where are people clicking when they get to your page? They can also measure the time users spend on a page. Nearly all of the tools we will mention in this chapter allow you to infer bounce rate, based on those two variables: You tell the tool what constitutes clicks off the page, and it will give you the statistics you need, such as the number of times that a user clicked off within the page without doing anything within three to six seconds (again, you set that threshold).

  What constitutes a high bounce rate is a matter of some debate. On advertising landing pages, the industry standard is to expect an 80 percent bounce rate. With paid search, we've all heard the 80/20 rule touted. That is, some partners have often said that we should be happy if only 80 percent of our external paid search referrals end in a bounce. But we want to change those expectations somewhat. If your paid and organic keywords for a page are all in the same cloud, you should expect much better results than the 80/20 rule. On your organic efforts, we encourage you to see anything more than a 50 percent bounce rate as unacceptable.

  Bounce rate by itself cannot help you understand *how* to make your pages more effective. When you encounter a high bounce rate, you will need to look at other data to analyze why you are attracting traffic outside of your target audience.

- **Referral data.** If users don't just type your URL into their browsers, you can assume that they clicked a link to get to your page. These links are divided into *internal* and *external* referrals. We will cover internal referrals in a later section.

  External referrals are very valuable because they indicate which owners of other sites find your content relevant. Most tools can gather the referring URL and other data about where visitors came from to get to your pages.

For our purposes, the most important external referrals are **search referrals**, when users land on your page by clicking on a search engine result. Not only are search referrals typically your highest volume of external referrals, but they can give you other information about what keywords are driving traffic to your pages.

The first place to look for analysis of why your bounce rate is high is search referral data. If you are getting a lot of traffic from Google and other search engines, but users then bounce off your page, you know that your keyword choice is problematic. Knowing how to fix it might require more referral data, along with doing additional keyword research (as described in Chapter 5).

Other external referral data is valuable because it shows which sites link to yours. If you analyze the content on these sites—such as audience, purpose, keyword data, and links—you can get a good sense of the make-up of other sites and know what your users also find relevant to them. Non-search external referrals are also an excellent source of potential link partners. If a site links to your pages and has a lot of other links on it, you can look into the other pages that it links to as being potentially relevant to your site.

- **Keyword data.** The most valuable data that tells you how to fix keyword problems comes from your keyword reports. Most analytics tools allow you to see not only the number of search referrals to a page, but which keywords users queried to get there. If a lot of users are coming to your page from queries containing variants of your keyword, and these same users have high bounce rates, you can use that information to zero in on the semantics of your keywords. Perhaps a particular keyword has a popular synonym. For example, if your keyword is *SOA* and you get a high bounce rate, it might mean that a lot of people from the Society of Actuaries clicked through to your page. So changing your keyword phrase to *Service Oriented Architecture* would lower your bounce rate.

  Sometimes finding out what keywords result in engagement is valuable. Not all your referrals will be from users who type a keyword that is in your page's title tag. If you find that you're getting a high bounce rate from users referred by your primary keyword, but that users referred from secondary keywords are engaging with your page, that tells you something: The content on your page does not match the keywords for which it was optimized very well.

- **Page audits.** Another reason users outside of your target audience might click your page when it appears in search listings is the short description. Google and other search engines show a two-line description of what users can expect to see when they click the link. If this description doesn't sufficiently cue readers as to the page's relevance to their search query, consider changing the two-line description (also known as the **description meta tag**). To use the same example as above, if your keyword is *SOA* and your description clearly states that the page is about *Service Oriented Architecture* rather than the *Society of Actuaries*, actuaries will be far less likely to click through to your page. Making sure that Google and other search engines display the correct short description is a good way to lower bounce rate (See Figure 9.1).

However, Google and other search engines can ignore the short description and continue to use an older one in their indexes. For this reason, it's also a good practice to write an eloquent content summary as the first two lines of your body copy. And make sure that your summary has your targeted keywords in it, preferably more than once.

Figure 9.1   A snippet of a Google Search Engine Results page (SERP) for the keyword "SOA." The short descriptions are the one and a half lines of black text below the link. Note that the text limit is 150 characters—slightly more than a Twitter post.

Tip: Use the `description` meta tag to indicate what you want search engines to display to users in the SERP. See Chapter 4 for other on-page factors that affect search ranking and the SERP display.

- **Engagement rate**. The opposite of bounce rate is **engagement rate:** the percentage of visitors (unique or otherwise) who click the links you want them to click on a page. If a visitor clicks on the links you want them to click on, it indicates that she finds the content relevant. You define what constitutes engagement, and your engagement parameters need not be black and white. Engagement can be defined as a continuum rather than an either/or proposition. Perhaps some links are especially high value: Users who click on those links will be engaging more deeply than those who click a navigation element to another page. The best engagement measurements delineate between types of engagement actions to help you better understand the degree of content relevance for the audience.

Case Study: Relating Engagement to Relevance

There are many ways of analyzing engagement data. Here is one way we are attempting to do it at IBM. We group the links on our Smarter Planet pages into two categories: calls to action on the topic-related page, and links to related Smarter Planet topics. Our operating assumption is that visitors who click the calls to action that we want them to click (such as to download a white paper, read the latest blog post, or watch a video) find the content on that page highly relevant. Visitors who click the persistent navigation links at the top or bottom of the page find the content on other pages within Smarter Planet relevant, but they won't necessarily find the content on that page relevant. They may click to go to other topics because they are looking for something other than what's on that page.

Figure 9.2 shows the types of links that we put on the Smart Planet pages.

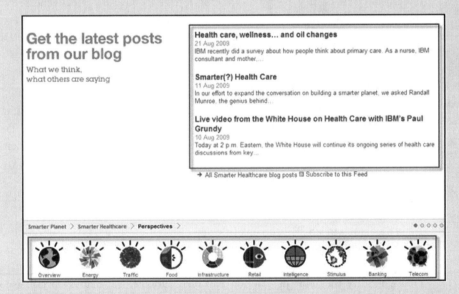

Figure 9.2   Two kinds of links on the Smarter Planet topic pages. The links in the red box constitute engagement with the topic on the page (Smarter Healthcare). Links in the blue box constitute engagement with the Smarter Planet site, though they are to other Smarter Planet topic pages.

- **Time on the page.** Not all pages are link-rich. In some cases, engagement can be defined in terms of how much time users spend on a site, typically measured in the average number of seconds or minutes per visit. However, the "time on a site" statistic is not universally respected, for two reasons.

    First, some users will come to your site and get distracted by other applications. Or they may get up and do something else away from the computer for awhile. In a typical scenario in the age of modern browsers such as Firefox, a user might open a folder full of bookmarks in tabs and only engage with a few of them. From a metrics perspective, the user was spending all her time on all of the tabs, when in reality she was only viewing one of the tabs at a time. And it's not uncommon for a user to spend all day on a page and never really engage with it. Because time on a site is measured in terms of the average time spent on a site for all users over a given time frame, this typical user behavior skews the averages for all visits. Most modern analytics programs throw out the outliers when they compile these averages. But not all do.

    Second, the other problem with time on a page is that it really only works for text-heavy pages without links. The goal of good page design is to get users to click desired links. If you rely on time on a page to measure effectiveness, you might be masking deeper issues with page design and site architecture. If all a user can do on a page is read, perhaps the best use for the page is to turn it into a PDF and link to it from another page.

- **Site overlays.** A **site overlay** is a screen capture that shows the percentage of visitors who clicked links on a given page (see Figure 9.3). Otherwise known as **heat maps,** these graphical representations of engagement give you at-a-glance views of what links are working and what links are not working on your pages. The assumption is that if a link is not working, users don't think it is relevant to them. So heat maps might not measure relevance for a page, but they will help you understand relevance for your links.

    Heat maps can tell you a lot about what needs to be fixed: Link anchor text, link positions, and many other factors influence whether users click links or not. As in the listing in a SERP, the link title and description should give users contextual cues as to what to expect if they click the link. If a link is not getting many clicks, change its anchor text, and take another heat map. If it still isn't getting clicks, modify the short description and take another heat map. If it still isn't working, modify the design to make the element more prominent on the page and take another heat map. This trial-and-error process helps you optimize the effectiveness of your links, one by one.

    Figure 9.3 shows an example of a heat map.

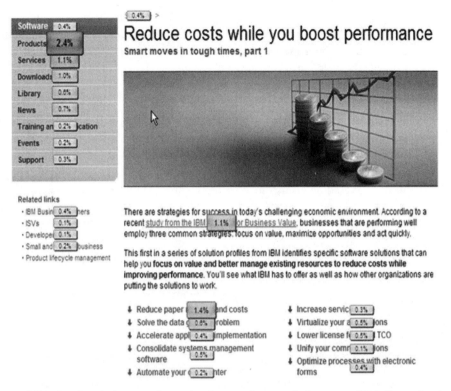

Figure 9.3 A snippet of an overlay or heat map of a page in ibm.com. Click-through rates are measured on each link on the page and displayed graphically to content owners.

- **Pathing data.** Heat maps can tell you what links are popular on a page. Internal referrals can tell you which links visitors have clicked on other pages within your site to get to a specific page. So the two measures give you a sense of link relevance at the page level. But many visitors will click multiple links on a site. These link paths can tell you about link relevance at the site level. The more links a visitor follows, the better your understanding of how users view the relevance of your pages to one another, and the greater the relevance of your site.

  Not all metrics packages can capture pathing data. Examples of companies that sell packages that capture pathing data include Unica and Omniture. But it can be some of the most important data to capture, especially if you have a complex site with a lot of interwoven content. Internal linking is key to site effectiveness, and an often-untapped source of link juice for your pages. Pathing data gives you a site-level view of how your links relate to one another from a user's perspective.

A lot of paths are only followed once. This doesn't tell you much, because users might follow a given path rather aimlessly. But if a path is followed multiple times, you can infer the relevance of link paths. You might need to look at link path data over a long period of time to get a large enough statistical sample, allowing you to make these inferences.

When you learn what paths are working and what paths are not, you can do all kinds of semantic analysis on the anchor text and the descriptions under the links to help understand why some paths are often followed and others are not. The aim is to induce your visitors to follow the relevant links so that they take your paths through the content. Pathing can also help you analyze how well your site does in guiding visitors to the content you want them to consume.

One caveat: Unlike in print publishing, on the Web, the visitor is in control. So no matter how much you try to funnel visitors through Web experiences, they will take paths of their choosing. You have to let go of control and let them take those paths. If user behavior shows that some paths are unexpectedly popular, that is not necessarily a bad thing. You can learn a lot about how your audience definitions differ from the audience that actually finds your content. And you can adjust to your audience by highlighting the popular paths.

Tools to Consider for your Metrics Tool Box

Everyone needs a good metrics tool box. Here are some useful tools, divided into three categories: Web Analytics tools, Search Metrics tools, and Content Quality metrics tools.

Web Analytics Tools

Webtrends. Offers the analytics and marketing optimization tasks that you perform most often: search engine marketing, Web site measurement, visitor analysis, and social media management. The company is a founding member of the Web Analytics Association and provides Web analytics for numerous global brands. It also offers Webtrends social measurements (www.webtrends.com/AboutWebTrends/Corporate-Background.aspx and www.webtrends.com/Products/WebTrendsOpenExchange/TargetingOptimization.aspx).

Coremetrics: Back in 2006, Coremetrics acquired the IBM SurfAid Analytics business. This tool provides actionable insights to visitor behavior and has analytic features for market optimization, merchandising and content analysis (www.coremetrics.com/).

Omniture's Site Catalyst. This Web analytics application is part of a suite of online business optimization offerings (see www.omniture.com/en/products/online_analytics/sitecatalyst). Another product offering, Omniture Discover, is promoted as an advanced Web analytics tool, allowing for data capture of deeper insights into your audience (www.omniture.com/en/products/online_analytics/discover).

Visitstat. As the name suggests, this Windows application is used to collect Web site visitor statistics through the use of server logs. It employs program filters to discern more detail about your audience (www.visitstat.com).

Webmetrics. This product offers simple-to-complex monitoring software provided by the flagship GlobalWatch platform, and related monitoring services (www.webmetrics.com/).

Unica NetInsight: This tool can give you all the data described in this chapter. It also plugs into other Unica analytics tools to help you capture data about transactions on your site, and to analyze data from an accounting standpoint (www.unica .com/products/enterprise-web-analytics.htm).

Search Metrics Tools

Covario: Automates much of the SEO processes that we highlight in this book, including page audits, link analysis, and social media engagement (www.covario .com/products_organic_search_insight.shtml).

Google Analytics: Offers integration with the Google AdWords and AdSense tools, integration with your site search, and segmentation, custom reports, and dashboards (http://www.google.com/analytics/features.html).

LSI Insights: A WordPress plug-in that can help you optimize your terminology for your audience. It is also a tool for keyword usage questions because it is said to mimic the way Google analyzes pages semantically (http://focustraffic.com/ lsi-products/lsi-insights-latent-semantic-indexing-research-226/).

Content Quality Metrics Tools

acrolinx IQ: Can be used at the authoring or post-publishing level to run quality reports and find the most pressing content quality problems in your environment (www.acrolinx.com/iq_overview_en.html).

Omniture's Test & Target product helps content teams increase content relevance by showing you how well their calls to action are working (www.omniture.com/ en/products/conversion/testandtarget).

Measuring Audience Semantics and Sentiment

Analyzing your audience is the first and most important step in creating relevant Web experiences. But if it's so important, why didn't we start with it in this chapter? Well, because Web audience analysis tools are typically more advanced and less commonplace than tools that can help you understand how relevant your content is to your visitors (whether they are in your target audience or not). We discussed at length how to analyze your audience through keyword research in Chapter 5. But keyword research is limited to short words and phrases. As we showed in Chapter 8, you also need to analyze social media settings to understand your audience's language preferences. This also requires **social media listening tools**, also known as **sentiment analysis tools**. Finally, the Web is not the only medium that your audience interacts with. You can gain insights about these offline media using traditional market intelligence techniques, such as surveys and focus groups.

Latent semantic indexing (LSI) is a statistical technique that identifies patterns in unstructured text (such as blog or Twitter text) and draws semantic conclusions from the patterns. LSI is based on the principle that meaning is contextual. If you can uncover the context by measuring the frequency of word groupings, you can determine the meaning. Unlike conventional keyword searches, LSI tends to do a better job of matching content to search queries, because it takes probable contexts into account.

LSI can be used to study your audience by helping you filter the unstructured text in social media settings by categories. You can use it to develop clouds of related posts or pages, all tagged with the assigned categories. If you look at these tag clouds, you will start to see relationships between the tags and can then base your keyword choices and terminology on the most relevant tags. This can also help you understand the topography of tag synonyms and other semantic relationships between tags.

LSI Insights (http://focustraffic.com/lsi-products/lsi-insights-latent-semantic-indexing-research-226) is a WordPress plug-in that can help you optimize your terminology for your audience. It is also a tool for keyword usage questions, because it is said to mimic the way Google analyses pages semantically.

Sentiment analysis, as it applies to social media, attempts to quantify the attitudes of writers in such social media settings as blogs, forums, Twitter, Facebook, and LinkedIn. It uses deep computational linguistics to determine the **polarity** of a blog or forum thread—whether it is positive, negative or neutral. You can scope the analysis to a particular blog or a whole network of blogs, forums, and discussion groups.

Sentiment analysis can help augment your semantic analysis of social media settings. Not only can you learn what words and phrases bloggers and others use to describe things, but you can know what the prevailing opinion is on a particular topic. Because your blog or Web site needs to persuade as well as inform, knowing your audience's disposition relative to key topics can help you craft persuasive arguments for them. Part of your job as a blogger is filling in the white space in the conversation. The easiest way to do this is by disagreeing with a popular opinion. But another way is to acknowledge that several top bloggers in your area have missed an angle that supports the prevailing opinion. Knowing what that prevailing opinion is, and where the gaps are, is crucial to your blogging success.

As we showed in Chapter 3, relevance is often defined in terms of two statements supporting each other in an argument. So, in general, the more persuasive your statements are, the more relevant they will seem to your audience.

Social Media Listening Tools

Social media listening, otherwise known as **social media mining**, is an emerging field that attempts to measure the sentiment and semantics around a set of topics. We profile three tools that can help your Web analytics people do this. Because the skills involved in running these tools and managing the data are rare, we recommend using a consulting service such as Converseon if you wish to perform social media mining. To get the most out of your social media mining strategy, it helps to consult with the experts in this emerging field.

Alterian (formerly known as Techrigy) SM2. SM2 pulls information from social media sites such as Twitter, Blogger, epinion, and Facebook. SM2 also tracks social bookmarking sites such as StumbleUpon, and Google's Knol. These feed into a distributed database with 10 billion pieces of user-generated content. SM2 lets you export these posts to Excel and then use any text analyzer tool, such as textSTAT, to see the relationships between words and associated keywords around the keyword phrase. This helps you craft your long-tail keywords and other phrases that your audience is likely to connect with.

Autonomy Optimost Adaptive Targeting. Adaptive Targeting mines audience attributes to create audience segments, including context (what we call *referral data*), geography, time of day, demographic information, and behavior. Once audience segments are created, multivariate tests are conducted on a variety of content ideas and layouts to determine the best solution for each audience segment. By using the tool's Intelligent Data Operating Layer (IDOL), writers, editors, and content strategists can better understand their audience. By leveraging IDOL, Optimost Adaptive Targeting now includes keyword clustering capabilities that identify concepts and patterns as they are emerging on the Web.

Converseon eResponder. Converseon is a social media mining consultancy that uses its eResponder tool to monitor and analyze conversations related to a given set of keywords. The tool can measure the sentiment of aggregate or individual posts, as well as determine how well a company is doing relative to competition in the blogosphere. It also measures the percentage of posts that are unbranded or not linked to any one company, which is a measure of the opportunity to gain "share of voice" for those conversations.

We mentioned traditional market intelligence techniques, such as surveys, in Chapter 5, but this information bears repeating here. It is important to have site surveys to get a better sense of your audience. But that will only help you understand the audience that finds your site. The goal is to grow your audience by reaching out to audience members with whom you have not yet connected. Social media is not the only way to do this. It's also helpful to conduct surveys that help you develop a sense of what other media your audience finds relevant. Perhaps a certain percentage of your audience members list a certain print journal among their regular offline reading. Learning these alternative venues is another way to understand your audience's expectations and preferences.

Note: It is not likely that regular radio listeners will correlate their activities with Web use. Because users type in things that they see much more often than they type in things that they hear, TV and other visual offline activities are much more likely to correlate with Web use than radio or other oral media. We have found this to be the case at IBM. When we run TV ads, we get strong correlating Web search data on the terms mentioned in the ads. When we run radio ads, we don't get nearly so much. This is just an extension of the media determinism theory we described in Chapter 2. This is an example of how offline activities can help you understand your online audiences.

Measuring Engagement Onsite and Offsite with PostRank

Some of your engagement will occur offsite—when external bloggers, Twitter users, and others link to and comment on your content away from your site. One good metric to measure the full range of engagement onsite and offsite is called PostRank (www.postrank.com/postrank). This metric is based on analysis of the 5 C's of engagement, in descending order of engagement strength:

- **Creating.** The strongest form of engagement is when a member of your audience writes a blog post or online article directly related to your content and links to it.

- **Critiquing.** This refers to that small percentage of blog readers who leave a comment: good, bad, or indifferent. This is still a very strong form of engagement with your content.

- **Chatting.** This refers to the act of posting a link on Facebook or otherwise sharing your content with like-minded people. It doesn't take as much effort as creating or critiquing, but it's still a very strong form of engagement.

- **Collecting.** This refers to bookmarking your site or subscribing to an RSS feed. It demonstrates the intent to become a repeat or routine visitor and is a somewhat weaker form than chatting.

The subjects of LSI, sentiment analysis, PostRank, and other social media market intelligence tools could fill entire books by themselves. We just want to give you some food for thought to enable you to work with your Web analytics and market intelligence colleagues and consultants to compile the best tool box for your environment. The more robust your metrics environment, the easier it will be to identify and target your audiences on the Web with rich, relevant content.

Summary

- One of the advantages of Web publishing is being able to make adjustments to content as circumstances change or you learn how well you are engaging with your audience.

- You don't measure relevance; you can infer it from a combination of measurements, including bounce rate and engagement rate. The assumption is, the more your customers engage with your site, the more relevant your content is to your target audience, and vice versa.

- No one Web analytics tool or suite is adequate to measuring everything you need. You will need Web analytics, content quality, and SEO effectiveness tools.

- A good way to learn more about your audience is to listen to social media conversations. The primary ways of doing this are LSI and sentiment analysis, which both use sophisticated linguistics to mine the unstructured text found in blogs and other social venues.

- LSI can be used to mine these sites for your audience's semantic preferences. Sentiment analysis can be used to mine these sites for audience attitudes.

- In addition to your online research, it is a good idea to conduct offline research to learn how your audience consumes media outside of the Web, and how that affects their attitudes and semantic preferences on the Web.

Bibliography

Alexandrou, Marios. "International SEO Keyword Research." *SEM and SEO Blog by Marios Alexandrou.* AllThingsSem.com, 5 Aug. 2007. www.allthingssem.com/international-seo-keyword-research.

Anderson, Chris. "The Long Tail." *Wired* Oct. 2004. www.wired.com/wired/archive/12.10/tail.html.

——. *The Long Tail: Why the Future of Business Is Selling Less of More.* New York: Hyperion, 2006.

Aristotle. *The Rhetoric and the Poetics of Aristotle.* Trans. W. Rhys Roberts. Intro. Edward P. J. Corbett. New York: Modern Library, 1984.

Austin, John L. *How to Do Things with Words.* London: Oxford UP, 1962.

——. *Philosophical Papers.* London: Oxford UP, 1961.

——. *Sense and Sensibilia.* London: Oxford UP, 1959.

Bailey, Matt. "Keyword Strategies—The Long Tail." *Search Engine Guide.* SearchEngineGuide .Com., 16 Aug. 2005. www.searchengineguide.com/matt-bailey/keyword-strategies-the-long-tail.php.

Baker, Gordon P. and Peter M. S. Hacker. *Wittgenstein: Meaning and Understanding.* Chicago: University of Chicago Press, 1985.

Berners-Lee, Tim and Mark Fischetti. *Weaving the Web: Origins and Future of the World Wide Web.* London: Orion Business, 1999.

Burge, Tyler. "Frege on Extensions of Concepts, From 1884 to 1903." *Philosophical Review* 93.1 (1984): 3-34.

——. "Individualism and the Mental." *Midwest Studies in Philosophy IV.* Ed. Peter A. French, Theodore E. Uehling, and Howard K. Wettstein. Minneapolis: University of Minnesota Press, 1979: 73-121.

——. "Semantical Paradox." *The Journal of Philosophy* 76 (1979): 169-98.

Burke, Kenneth. A Grammar of Motives. Berkeley: University of California Press, 1969.

——. A Rhetoric of Motives. Berkeley: University of California Press, 1969.

Bush, Vennevar. "As We May Think." *Atlantic Monthly* July 1945. www.theatlantic.com/doc/194507/bush.

Chomsky, Noam. *Aspects of the Theory of Syntax.* Cambridge, MA: MIT Press. 1965.

——. *Cartesian Linguistics.* New York: Harper and Row, 1966.

——. *Knowledge of Language: Its Nature, Origin and Use.* New York: Harcourt Brace Jovanovich, 1986.

——. *Language and Mind.* New York: Harcourt Brace Jovanovich, 1968.

——. *Syntactic Structures.* The Hague: Mouton, 1957.

Clement, Richard W. "Medieval and Renaissance Book Production—Manuscript Books." *The Online Reference Book of Medieval Studies* 2008. www.the-orb.net/encyclop/culture/books/medbook1.html.

Cummings, E. E. *Complete Poems.* New York: Harcourt Brace Jovanovich, 1972.

Davidson, Donald. *Truth and Interpretation.* Oxford: Clarendon Press, 1984.

deGeyter, Stoney. "Comprehensive Guide to Keyword Research, Selection & Organization, Part I." *SearchEngineGuide.* Search Engine Guide, 8 October 2008. www.searchengineguide.com/stoney-degeyter/comprehensive-guide-to-keyword-research.php.

Duranti, Alessandro. *Linguistic Anthropology.* Cambridge: Cambridge UP, 1997.

Eisenstein, Elizabeth. *The Printing Press as an Agent of Change.* Cambridge: Cambridge UP, 1983.

——. *The Printing Revolution in Early Modern Europe.* Cambridge: Cambridge UP, 1983.

Faigley, Lester. "Nonacademic Writing: The Social Perspective." *Writing in Nonacademic Settings.* Ed. Lee Odell and Dixie Goswami. New York: Guliford, 1985. 231-248.

Fishkin, Rand, "Search Engine Ranking Factors 2009." *SEO—Search Engine Optimization.* SEOmoz, 2009. www.seomoz.org/article/search-ranking-factors.

Flower, Linda. "Cognition, Context, and Theory Building." *College Composition and Communication* 40 (1989): 282-311.

——. "A Cognitive Process Theory of Writing." *College Composition and Communication* 32 (1981): 365-387.

——. *The Construction of Negotiated Meaning: A Social Cognitive Theory of Writing.* Carbondale, IL: Southern Illinois UP, 1994.

——. "The Dynamics of Composing: Making Plans and Juggling Constraints." *Cognitive Processes in Writing.* Ed. Lee W. Gregg and Erwin R. Steinberg. Hillsdale, NJ: Erlbaum, 1980. 31-50.

——. *Problem-Solving Strategies for Writing, Third Edition.* New York: Harcourt Brace Jovanovich, 1985.

—— and John R. Hayes. "The Cognition of Discovery: Defining a Rhetorical Problem." *College Composition and Communication* 31 (1980): 21-32.

Foucault, Michel. *The Archeology of Knowledge and the Discourse on Language.* Trans. A. M. Sheridan Smith. New York: Pantheon-Random, 1972.

Frege, Gottlob. "On Sense and Reference." *Translations from the Philosophical Writings of Gottlob Frege.* Trans. and Ed. P. Geach and M. Black. Oxford: Blackwell, 1952, 1960.

——. "The Thought: A Logical Inquiry." *Mind* 65.259 (1956): 289-311.

Gibson, David, Jon Kleinberg, and Prabhaker Raghavan. "Inferring Web Communities from Link Topology." *Proceedings of the Ninth ACM Conference on Hypertext and Hypermedia,* 1998. www.cs.cornell.edu/home/kleinber/ht98-comm.pdf.

Glover, Eric. "The 'Real World' Web Search Problem." *Videolectures.* VideoLectures.Net, n.d. http://videolectures.net/mmdss07_glover_trw.

Grice, H. P. "Meaning." *Philosophical Review* 66 (1957): 377-88.

——. "Utterer's Meaning and Intentions." *Philosophical Review* 78 (1969): 147-77.

——. "Utterer's Meaning, Sentence Meaning, and Word Meaning." *Foundations of Language* 4 (1968): 225-42.

"Homonym." *Wikipedia, the Free Encyclopedia.* Wikimedia Foundation, Inc., n.d. http://en .wikipedia.org/wiki/Homonyms.

"How to Find and Target Long Tail Keywords for More Search Engine Traffic." *Dosh Dosh.* Dosh Dosh, n.d. www.doshdosh.com/how-to-target-long-tail-keywords-increase-search-traffic.

Joyce, Michael. "No One Tells You This: Secondary Orality and Hypertextuality." *Oral Tradition* 17.2 (2002): 325-345. http://journal.oraltradition.org/files/articles/17ii/Joyce.pdf.

Katz, J. J. *Semantic Theory.* New York: Harper and Row, 1972.

Kleinberg, Jon M. "Authoritative Sources in a Hyperlinked Environment." *IBM Research Report RJ 10076, May 1997.* An extended version is available in *Journal of the ACM,* 46.5 (Sept. 1999): 604-632.

Kripke, Saul. "Naming and Necessity." *The Semantics of Natural Language.* Ed. D. Davidson and G. Harmon. Dordrecht: Reidel 1972.

——. *Wittgenstein on Rules and Private Language.* Cambridge, MA: Harvard UP, 1982.

Krug, Steven. *Don't Make Me Think, A Common Sense Approach to Web Usability.* Circle.com Library, 2000.

Lamb, Gregory. "How the Web Changes Your Reading Habits." *Christian Science Monitor* 23 June 2005. www.csmonitor.com/2005/0623/p13s02-stin.html.

"The Latest News Headlines—Your Vote Counts." *Project for Excellence in Journalism (PEJ).* Journalism.org, 12 Sep. 2007. www.journalism.org/node/7493.

Levi-Strauss, Claude. *The Savage Mind,* Chicago: University of Chicago Press, 1966.

McGee, Matt. "Search Queries Are Getting Longer: Hitwise Report." *Search Engine Land.* Search Engine Land, 24 Feb. 2009. http://searchengineland.com/search-queries-getting-longer-16676.

McLuhan, Marshall. *The Gutenberg Galaxy: The Making of the Typographic Man.* Toronto: University of Toronto Press, 1962.

——. *The Medium is the Message.* New York: Bantam, 1967.

——. *Understanding Media, The Extensions of Man.* New York: McGraw-Hill, 1964.

Monk, Ray. *Wittgenstein: The Duty of Genius.* London: Vintage, 1991.

Moran, Mike and Bill Hunt. *Search Engine Marketing Inc.: Driving Traffic to Your Company's Web Site.* New York: IBM Press, 2005.

——. *Search Engine Marketing Inc.: Driving Traffic to Your Company's Web Site, 2nd Edition.* New York: IBM Press, 2009.

Moore, Bill. "Homograph, Homonym, or Homophone?" *EzineArticles Submission.* EzineArticles .com, n.d. http://ezinearticles.com/?Homograph,-Homonym,-or-Homophone?&id=275667.

Nielsen, Jakob. *Designing Web Usability: The Practice of Simplicity*. Indianapolis: New Riders Press, 1999.

——. "How Little Do Users Read." *How Little Do Users Read (Jacob Nielsen's Alertbox)*. UseIt.Com, 6 May 2008. www.useit.com/alertbox/percent-text-read.html.

——. "How Users Use the Web." *Reading on the Web (Alertbox)*. Useit.Com, 1 Oct. 2007. www.useit.com/alertbox/9710a.html.

——. *Hypertext and Hypermedia*. Boston: Academic Press, 1990.

——. *Usability Engineering*. Boston: Academic Press, 1993.

——. "Write for Reuse." *Write for Reuse (Jakob Nielsen's Alertbox)*. UseIt.Com, 2 Mar. 2009. www.useit.com/alertbox/writing-reuse.html.

——. "Writing Styles for Print vs. Web." *Writing Style for Print vs. Web (Jakob Nielsen's Alertbox)*. UseIt.Com, 9 June 2008. www.useit.com/alertbox/print-vs-online-content.html.

——. and Hoa Loranger. *Prioritizing Web Usability*. Indianapolis: New Riders Press, 2006.

—— and Marie Tahir. *Homepage Usability: 50 Websites Deconstructed*. Indianapolis: New Riders Press, 2006.

Nystrand, Martin. "Rhetoric's 'Audience' and Linguistics' 'Speech Community': Implications for Understanding Writing, Reading, and Text." *What Writers Know: The Language, Process and Structure of Written Discourse*. Ed. Martin Nystrand. New York: Academic Press, 1982. 1-28.

Ong, Walter, SJ. *Orality and Literacy: The Technologizing of the Word*. London: Routledge 1982.

——. "The Writer's Audience Is Always a Fiction." *PMLA* 90.1 (1975): 9-21.

Peterson, Constance J. "Writing for a Web Audience." *Smartisans.com*. SoftMedia Artisans, Inc., 2001. www.smartisans.com/articles/web_writing.aspx.

Pike, Walter. "Writing for Social Media Is NOT the Same." *Marketing and Media in South Africa*. Bizcommunity.com, 2 Jul. 2008. www.bizcommunity.com/Article/196/16/25990.html.

Porter, James E. *Audience and Rhetoric*. Englewood Cliffs, NJ: Prentice Hall, 1992.

Quine, W. *Word and Object*. Cambridge, MA: MIT Press, 1960.

"relevant >> relevance." *Google Notebook*. Google, n.d. www.google.com/notebook/public/0749126161992010151l/BDRreIgoQ853VyIsi.

Saenger, Paul. *Space Between Words, the Origins of Silent Reading*. Palo Alto, CA: Stanford UP 1997.

Saleem, Muhammad. "Writing for the Social Media Everyman." *Writing for the Social Media Everyman | Copyblogger*. Copyblogger LLC, n.d. www.copyblogger.com/writing-for-social-media.

Searle, John R. "A Classification of Illocutionary Acts." *Language in Society* 5.1 (1976): 1-23.

——. *Intentionality: An Essay in the Philosophy of Mind*. Cambridge: Cambridge UP, 1983.

——. *Speech Acts, an Essay in the Philosophy of Language*. Cambridge: Cambridge UP, 1969.

Selzer, Jack. "What Constitutes a 'Readable' Technical Style?" *New Essays in Technical and Scientific Communication: Research, Theory, Practice*. Ed. Paul V. Anderson et al. Farmingdale, NY: Baywood Press, 1983. 71-89.

Sperber, Dan and Deirdre Wilson. *Relevance: Communication and Cognition*. Cambridge, MA: Harvard UP, 1986.

Strawson, P. F. "Identifying Reference and Truth Values." *Theoria* 3 (1964): 96-118.

———. "Intention and Convention in Speech Acts." *Philosophical Review* 73 (1964): 439-60.

———. *Logico-Linguistic Papers.* London: Methuen, 1971.

Strunk, William Jr. and E. B. White. *The Elements of Style.* 3rd ed. Boston: Allyn & Bacon, 1979.

Tarski, Alfred. *Logic, Semantics, Mathematics.* Oxford: Clarendon Press, 1956.

Travis, Charles. "On What Is Strictly Speaking True." *Canadian Journal of Philosophy* 15.22 (1985): 187-229.

———. *The True and the False: The Domain of the Pragmatic.* Amsterdam: J. Benjamin, 1981.

———. *The Uses of Sense: Wittgenstein's Philosophy of Language.* Oxford: Clarendon Press, 1989.

Vlastos, Gregory. *Socrates, Ironist and Moral Philosopher.* Ithaca, NY: Cornell UP, 1991.

Wall, Aaron. "Google Semantically Related Words & Latent Semantic Indexing Technology." *SEO Book.com.* seobook.com, 3 Feb. 2005. www.seobook.com/archives/000657.shtml.

Weinreich, Harald, Hartmut Obendorf, Eelco Herder, and Matthias Mayer: "Not Quite the Average: An Empirical Study of Web Use." *ACM Transactions on the Web 2.1* (Feb. 2008): Article 5, 5:1-5:31.

"What is Unicode?" *Unicode Consortium.* The Unicode Consortium, n.d. http://unicode.org/standard/WhatIsUnicode.html.

Wittgenstein, Ludwig. *Blue and Brown Book.* 2nd ed. New York: Harper Collins, 1960.

———. *On Certainty.* Ed. G. E. M. Anscomb and G. H. von Wright. Trans. Anscomb. New York: Harper Collins, 1969.

———. *Philosophical Grammar.* Ed. Rush Rhees. Trans. Anthony Kennedy. Berkeley: University of California Press, 1978.

———. *Philosophical Investigations.* 3rd ed. London: Macmillan 1989.

———. *Philosophical Remarks.* Ed. Rush Rhees. Trans. Raymond Hargraves and Roger White. Chicago: University of Chicago Press, 1975.

———. *Remarks on the Philosophy of Psychology, Vol. I.* Ed. G. E. M. Anscomb and G. H. von Wright. Trans. Anscomb. Chicago: University of Chicago Press, 1980.

———. *Remarks on the Philosophy of Psychology, Vol. II.* Ed. G. E. M. Anscomb and G. H. von Wright. Trans. Anscomb. Chicago: University of Chicago Press, 1980.

———. *Tractatus Logico-Philosophicus.* Trans. D. F. Pears and B. F. McGinness. London: Routledge and Kegan Paul, 1961.

———. *Zettel.* Ed. G. E. M. Anscomb and G. H. von Wright. Trans. Anscomb. Berkeley: University of California Press, 1967.

Young, Richard E., Alton L. Becker, and Kenneth L. Pike. *Rhetoric: Discovery and Change.* New York: Harcourt Brace Jovanovich, 1970.

INDEX

FREE Online Edition

Your purchase of **Audience, Relevance, and Search** includes access to a free online edition for 120 days through the Safari Books Online subscription service. Nearly every IBM Press book is available online through Safari Books Online, along with more than 5,000 other technical books and videos from publishers such as Addison-Wesley Professional, Cisco Press, Exam Cram, O'Reilly, Prentice Hall, Que, and Sams.

SAFARI BOOKS ONLINE allows you to search for a specific answer, cut and paste code, download chapters, and stay current with emerging technologies.

Activate your FREE Online Edition at www.informit.com/safarifree

> **STEP 1:** Enter the coupon code: TSEUQGA.

> **STEP 2:** New Safari users, complete the brief registration form.
> Safari subscribers, just log in.

If you have difficulty registering on Safari or accessing the online edition, please e-mail customer-service@safaribooksonline.com